Darren Yost

IDENTITY SHIFT

Crossing Over to Kingdom

May God bless you and your may your life be prosperous.

Amanda L. Brothers

Amanda Brothers

Follow me on social media!

facebook.com/amanda.kellybrothers
facebook.com/bewholenow

Instagram: albrothers13

Identity Shift: Crossing Over to Kingdom

For publishing information contact,
Amanda L. Brothers
Empowered For Change, LLC

Cover Design by Karen Captline
www.betterbecreative.com

Printed in the United States of America
Amanda Brothers, Empowered For Change, LLC

ISBN: 978-0-578-37108-5

ACKNOWLEGEMENTS

I dedicate this book to my biggest cheerleader, friend, and husband, Steven, to our five children, LaQuita, Rika (Tyquail), Kiara, and Zachary, to our eight beautiful grand-blessings, Kamari, Azaria, Ny'Ari, Tyquail, ZiYanna, Asaad, Libi, and Sherrod and to the memory of our ninth grand-blessing Lily June. You all are my inspiration. You are my WHY in life. I love you all dearly and thank God for each of you. You bring so much joy to my life. I pray for His choicest blessing over each of your lives.

I would also like to acknowledge and thank some special people in my life. First, a huge thank you to my husband Steven for your patience while I was writing this book. Thank you for listening and giving your feedback. I honor you and value all that you bring to our life together.

To my friends Adele Georges and Tracey Veney for allowing me to read to you so that I could get a better idea of the flow and for always being there when I need to talk.

Kaaren Poole, for being my accountability partner. You inspired me, motivated me, and encouraged me each week to keep going.

Beverly Walthour, Business Strategist, Coach, and author, is my business coach and beta reader for this book. You have been such a blessing in my life. You are an amazing woman of God, a great coach, a woman of integrity, and I value your friendship and guidance in my life and business. You give so unselfishly and inspire me, encourage me, you push me, you don't accept mediocrity.

Allison Garcia, author, you have been such tremendous support during my journey as a new author. Thank you for your encouragement during my quest, for being a beta reader for this book and giving your valuable feedback, for accepting me into your writers' group, and for introducing me to a community of other amazing authors.

Aaron Gordon, (author), thank you for encouraging me during my journey to becoming a new author and for being a beta reader for this book. You were always willing to answer questions for me. You inspire me with your wisdom and ability to give thought-provoking messages that transform lives. Thank you for being the man of God you are and making the impact in the world that you do. Keep allowing God to use you.

Wes and Cindy Dove, authors, Dove Development and Consulting. You have been supportive of me and my personal development since the day we met. I am grateful for your friendship and willingness to be beta readers for this book. Your encouragement and feedback are invaluable. You two have a genuine heart for what you do. You are impacting and changing many lives, including mine.

And, Regina Rushing, author, for your encouragement and the valuable feedback you gave during my journey to become a new author. I am grateful for all of the guidance that you provided to me.

TABLE OF CONTENTS

1

INTRODUCTION

When God planted the idea for this book in my spirit, I wrote down the topic and put it aside for about 15 years. I would take a few notes every now and then but I didn't feel as though I was the most appropriate person to tackle this subject. My mindset at the time was, who am I to write a book about our identity in Christ? I felt very inadequate. I wasn't confident in who I was in Christ.

I'm being transparent here because I want to help those who are reading this. I was already a minister of the gospel, called by God to the office of evangelist. I was licensed into the ministry in 1996 and ordained in 1999. I felt very strongly that God called me and wanted me to do this but because I did not yet fully understand my identity in Christ, it was at times very challenging and difficult to embrace and walk in. You see, I discovered that I not only had the wrong view of who I was but I also had the wrong view of who God is. I saw God as this hard task master. I saw God as someone who was going to send me to Hell if I didn't do everything right. I thought I had to beg Him for everything - His mercy, forgiveness, to meet my needs, everything. I thought I had to be perfect. Although I knew that I could not earn my salvation, I lived every day as if I did. I didn't see God as a loving, gracious Father. I didn't see Him as my victory over death and Hell. I didn't see Him as my life-giver and my provision in life. I didn't see Him as He truly is. Therefore, I did not see myself as I truly was and now am in Him. I did not understand what it truly meant to be in covenant with Him nor did I understand the transition to kingdom that had taken place. Why? because I didn't take responsibility to learn and seek out the truth for myself. I listened to those that were teaching a gospel of hate, a gospel of works, a fire and brimstone gospel and that shook my faith and gave me a very negative image of God's character. It was very rare for me to hear people teach about a God of love, God as a good Father, or that God desires to have relationship with us.

I am blessed that God led me to some amazing pastors that taught a gospel of love. They taught about the kingdom of God and not just salvation. They nurtured and supported me. It helped to change the tainted perception that I had of who God is. Even though I had some great pastors and they taught me the truth of God's word, it was still easy for me to be drawn away and to get caught up in untruth because I didn't always seek out the truth for myself.

The point that I want to make is that, it was my responsibility to open the book and study for myself and not rely on what others preached and taught. With the guidance of the Holy Spirit, He could give me the interpretation and understanding of His word that I desperately needed. It was my responsibility to develop my own personal relationship with God. It was my personal responsibility to learn the truth about who God is and who I am in Him. No one else.

Honestly, I'm still growing into who I am in Him. Based on my personal experience, people will train you on the protocols, procedures, and rituals of how to be religious according to their denomination but very little about being in relationship with a living God. What I have discovered after years of trial and error is that ultimately it was my responsibility to learn how to study the bible and to study it for myself. It was also my responsibility to develop my personal relationship with God, to pray and seek God's will and direction for my life. I was responsible for learning who I am in Christ and who He is in me. Yes, I felt that needed to be repeated because you have the same responsibility. Listening to and believing everything that's taught and preached without researching it for yourself is dangerous. There are life and death consequences attached. So, as you read this book don't just take what I say as gospel. Please, please take responsibility to learn for yourself. Study your bible, invite the Holy Spirit into your study time, learn to hear and recognize God's voice so that you can be equipped with the truth.

As I continued to learn and grow, I ran out of excuses as to why I couldn't write this book. There was no one to blame for not completing this book but me, especially since God led two people to prophecy to me that I am supposed to be writing. Therefore, it became time for me to finally get this book done.

As a child of God, if you get nothing else out of this, please understand that it is up to you to take personal responsibility for developing and growing in who you are in Christ and seeking out a personal and intimate relationship with God. Don't allow yourself to do what we so often do, which is relying on other people and playing the blame game because that is where we get into trouble. What if they (those that we are listening to and relying on) are wrong? What if they have no real relationship with God? What if they are interpreting the bible based on what they heard from someone else who interpreted it based on what they heard or learned from someone else? Get where I'm going with this? Yet this is what people do every day. God can give you a specific word through other people and He does at times but that's not what I'm talking about here. I'm talking about relying on others and ultimately building our relationship with God, or lack thereof, with what we see and hear from other people instead of going to the source Himself.

What does this have to do with our identity you ask? Everything. You see, how we interpret the word of God is important to our identity. The bible is our guidebook. It is the will and testament that was left for us to follow so that we can have and enjoy life (Hebrews 9:16-17). It teaches us who we really are, how we came into being, who our Father is, what our role in life is, and what our inheritance is. In it we also learn how to live while we are in the world, how to access the promises of God as children of God, how to be victorious in spiritual warfare, as well as many other things pertaining to life and godliness. It is the basic gospel, which consist of more than just getting saved and going to heaven someday. The Bible is full of God's wisdom and His promises to us. It is our roadmap to a life of victory in Him. We can't find that victory any other way no matter where we look or how hard we try.

Again, I learned this the hard way. But I did learn, and am continuing to grow in that knowledge. I will continue to learn and grow as long as I am alive and breathing on this side of heaven. God wants us all to know who we are in Him and He doesn't make it hard, we do. We as a people have been deceived into believing that the bible is hard to understand so people fail to study it. The world system has deceived us into believing that we are who other people say we are or perceive us to be. We live our lives following our emotions or allowing fear, and other people, to control us. Over reliance on emotions, fear, and listening to the wrong people leads to deception. That is why God's word tells us to walk by faith and not by sight. Sometimes what we see, and what we feel can lead us astray. It does not always reveal what is really going on behind the scenes or beneath the surface.

I didn't understand all of this when God planted this book in my spirit. I still needed to go through a process of renewing my mind. So often we believe that when God gives us an assignment or plants something in our spirits, we are supposed to do it at that very moment, but that is not always the case. Remember, I shared that it's been about 15 years. For years I felt guilty. For years I felt not good enough and that I was disappointing God because I was not writing. I felt that way because I didn't know I could ask Him questions about what He wanted me to do with what He had given me. I didn't understand my identity as a child of God. I didn't understand what it meant to have a relationship with God. I didn't even know that there was such a "thing." It was rare to hear people talking about having a relationship with God. The preaching and teaching that I was accustomed to was about salvation, going to heaven, or going to Hell due to my flaws and behaviors. And guess what? I fell right in line with what was already being preached and taught. I didn't know any better.

This journey from where I was to where I am now has not been easy. I've experienced a lot and in it I've learned a lot about my true identity in Christ, who God is and how faithful and loving He truly is. I've learned that identity encompasses more than my name and the roles that I hold in society. It's about a lot more than what I do, where I live, or what I have or don't have. It has nothing to do with what people think of me, whether they like me or not, accept me or not, how they treat me, what they say about me or don't say about me, or their opinion or perception of me. Believe it or not, my identity has nothing to do with how I feel about myself or my own perception of who I am or am not. What really matters when it comes to my identity and yours for that matter is who God says that you are. We came into this world with an identity. We were created with purpose in mind. We were given gifts, talents, personality and characteristics that are unique to each one of us individually. There is no one on earth that has my fingerprint or footprint, there is no one that was created to fulfill my purpose the way that I can and there is no one that can make an impact in the world quite like I can. The same holds true for you. We all have been given our own unique identity, purpose, and assignment. It's all a part of our identity.

Everything I went through has taught me some valuable lessons, helped me to grow and has shown me just how important it is to know my identity based on who God says I am and to have a relationship with Him. My journey in life has taught me that my Christianity is not about religion and religion can't help me. This journey that I am on is all about relationship with the Father, it's all about covenant and it's all about the kingdom. All that I have learned and experienced has truly changed the trajectory of my life.

"As of May 2019, there are 7.7 billion people in the world." (https://www.worldometers.info/world-population). Every person that exists in the world is here by divine design. Every person has a specific purpose for their existence. There is not one person here that is here by mistake or happenstance. This includes you. There are also several different major religions in the world with several different denominations that fall under some of them.

Christianity is the largest of the major religions with "more than 2.3 billion people that practice some form of Christianity" (http://worldpopulationreview.com/countries/most-christian-countries). But this is not about religion. This is about relationship, relationship as it relates to our identity and our purpose in life and in Christ.

Most people in the world are unable to articulate who they truly are, why they are here, where they come from, where they are going when this life is over or how to get there. They may have been practicing their religion for years or maybe professing to be Christians for years but never knew that a relationship is what is needed in order to discover and truly live the abundant life that Jesus spoke of. If you are unable to answer these questions, trust me, you will go aimlessly through life never accomplishing anything of value. And I believe you will live an empty, unfulfilled, and defeated life, even if you are very successful according to the world's standards. Jesus said ...

"I am the way, and the truth, and the life. No one comes to the Father except through me" (ESV, Jn. 14:6).

The word of God also says, *"For what shall it profit a man, if he shall gain the whole world, and lose his own soul"* (KJV, Mark 8:36).

Take a moment here to reflect on the questions I asked above and write down your answers. Don't go from head knowledge or what sounds good but be very honest with yourself and write what you truly believe in your heart.

____

____

____

____

____

____

____

This book is meant to take you the believer in Christ on a journey, showing you why it's important to know who you are, what important elements are necessary to you discovering who you are and what the bible says about who you are so that you can live the life that God originally planned for you to live. My prayer is that as you read this book it will spark a desire in you to dig even deeper into the scriptures to learn more about who you are and birth a deeper desire to build a more intimate relationship with our Great Creator and Father, His Son Jesus and the Holy Spirit. All three have very important roles in our lives. My hope is also that you will be ready to make that Identity Shift and Crossover into the kingdom of God. So, let's begin our journey into learning who we are in Christ and the benefits of shifting our identity for the one He always intended.

2

JOURNEY TO DISCOVERY

All of our lives, we have been on a journey. A journey of discovering who we are. We are trying to make sense of and figure out the meaning of life and the role we are to play in it. As we learn and grow through this thing called life, we discover and develop what we refer to as our identity. We don't focus on it, but we are created with our own unique identity. And because we don't focus on it, we don't think about actually sitting down and doing a deep dive into who we are. What is it that we like or dislike and why? What is it that we want to do or not do? What have we been through in life, and what has it taught us? How do our experiences in life play into our calling and assignments in life? Why do we think the way we think, feel the way we feel, or believe the things we believe? and where is God in all of it? What brings us joy? What do we desire to have in and out of life? Why are we here? etc. All of this is important to know, but so many people just let life happen or do what others want them to do and believe that they have to go along with it. Doing this deep dive and understanding your past and how it has affected you and what role it has played in where you find yourself today is vital if you are ever going to be successful in life. Outside of seeking God, doing the inner work is the next most important step you can take when you are seeking to understand your true identity. When doing this deep dive, it is important to pray and seek God for His truth.

As children, someone made decisions for us (parents, guardians), told us what to do and think, but as adults, we have choices, and we get to make decisions for ourselves.

We can make changes and adjust things as we see fit. God gave us free will and with that comes the right to choose and make decisions.

When we are born, we are given a name by our parents. The name we answered to throughout our lives. Some of us had nicknames. Some of us were called inappropriate names. These are the names by which we identify and the person we believe ourselves to be, but who is that person? What does it mean to be the name we answer to? That which we become is predicated by that which we are taught, that which we observe, that which we experience, or that which we choose. Proverbs 23:7 tells us that "As a man thinks in his heart, so is he." It means whatever you believe and think about yourself, that is who and what you are. It doesn't matter who God says you are or who He created you to be if you don't know it or believe it. What are your thoughts about yourself?

Take another moment and jot down some ideas you have about who you believe yourself to be?

____

____

____

____

____

____

Now I challenge you to take a few moments and go through the scriptures to see what God says about you. Does what He said align with what you say? If not, allow God's truth about you to become your reality.

We are always learning and becoming. Everything we learn that we allow to become a belief becomes a part of us whether we know it or not. I've said this before, everything we believe becomes the basis of every decision we make in life. We develop a belief system that dictates the person we grow up to be, the things we do, and the way we navigate life. In the midst of all of this, we make the mistake of confusing who we are with what we do, and it causes what we do to become who we are.

We are all at different stages in our lives. We grew up differently and have experienced different things in life. Our journeys are all different. We have different perspectives of what life and the pursuit of a good and meaningful life are. We are all unique and because of this, we all see things differently.

Some grew up in Christian homes, and some did not. Some were raised in the church. Some were not. Some were raised to have good moral values, treat others with kindness, and do the right thing. Some were not. All of this helped to shape who and what we believe we are and has designed our belief systems.

There is so much that we have learned about the world's way of doing things that we have to unlearn as we begin our walk as new creations in Christ. It starts with renewing our minds through the word of God (Romans 12:1-2). When we start to understand that as new creations in Christ, we are no longer resident citizens of this world, but we become citizens of the kingdom of God, life begins to take on a brand-new meaning (Eph. 2: 4-7). We are here to continue the work that Jesus started in the world (John 17:14-21).

Some have accepted Jesus' finished work on the cross and have made Jesus, Lord, and Savior of their lives and have developed a real relationship with Him. Some believe that they are born again but never learned that it's not just about salvation but a relationship with God through Jesus Christ and not just about going to heaven someday. Still, some are not born again, and they know nothing about God but that which those that profess to know God have lived or shared, and they want no part of it based on their perception of what it is all about because of what they have heard or seen.

Now, I'm not condemning anyone. This book is not about bashing or pointing fingers or making anyone feel bad. It's not about modifying anyone's behavior or getting people to act or live a certain way. It's not about religion or religious practices. This book is all about identity and the importance of relationship as it relates to our identity in Christ. It's written to help you understand your true identity in Christ and be equipped to decide on making that Identity Shift. My desire is for you to be empowered by God, His Word (Jesus), and the Holy Spirit and finally embrace who you are in Him, crossover into the kingdom, and start living the life you were meant to live.

Every experience in our lives, is meaningful. It teaches us things about ourselves that we would have never known if we had not had that experience. I believe it also teaches us things about God, that had we not had those experiences, we would have never known. I've learned that it's crucial to pay attention to the things that happen in my life and ask questions so that I can learn from them and grow. I've also learned that *"...all things [truly do] work together for good to those that love God, to those that are called according to His purpose"* (NKJV, Rom. 8:28).

As I continue to grow and mature in my walk with the Lord, I discover there is so much more to this journey called life than I ever realized. Talk about clueless! I had no idea. My perception of what life was supposed to be was created by my little boxed-in, limited experiences in life. You see, I allowed society to choose the life I was living based on how I perceived my little sphere of it. I'm sure that if you are honest with yourself, you have probably done the same thing and quite possibly are still living in that place as well, but God had a different plan for me, He has a different plan and call for your life as well. His word tells us that...

> *"Eye has not seen, nor ear heard, nor have entered into the heart of man the things which God has prepared for those who love Him"*

(NKJV, 1 Cor. 2:9) and *"[He knows] the plans [He]ha[s] for you, declares the Lord, plans for welfare and not for evil, to give you a future and a hope"* (ESV, Jer. 29:11).
He has a good plan for each of us.

My journey in life has brought me to a place where I now realize the importance of truly understanding who I am and what I want in life instead of just letting life happen to me. I've discovered over the years that I have the power to create the life that I desire to live, but first, I have to know who I am to discover what I truly want and how to manifest those things in my life. Praying and seeking God is crucial in the process. His word tells me that He has plans for me and, I most certainly want His plans for my life. As I was seeking God about my life this led me to develop a program called "Personalized Victory Roadmap." I am currently working on turning it into a course. Its purpose is to first of all shift our mindsets from trying to fit God into our lives to incorporating our lives into our relationship with God.. It will also help us evaluate where we are, discover what we want our lives to look like, and then map out a plan to get us there. We focus on 9 areas of life to include our overall quality of life and start to create action steps to get us to where we desire to be. This is my way of working on bringing harmony to every area of my life and staying focused as I continue my journey to walk out the plans that God has for me as He continues to reveal. I also have a mentor who has taken me through the process of doing an even deeper dive into my identity, purpose, and assignments in life. God is very strategic and He has led me to the coaches and mentors that are helping me to create the life that I desire for myself and to walk out the plans that He has for me. I had to learn to invest in myself because I don't believe that we are meant to do life alone. There are people attached to us and we are created for relationships.

I truly believe that there are others just like I used to be, that have allowed life to just happen. You have no idea about your true identity, what you want, or how to have the life you vaguely see for yourself. I believe that receiving our answers has to start with seeking God. I mean really seeking God, understanding that He is our Creator, our Source for everything we require, and anything outside of Him is a resource. Then, you must be willing to do some internal work and examine your life. You have to be willing to come face to face with those areas that you would rather not look at and acknowledge, learn from them, and confront them before you can conquer them. We all have wounds, broken places, and pains from our past that we are yet to deal with. It is not just you. It's time to allow God into those places and begin your healing process. No guilt or condemnation just open honest examination.

As believers in Christ, understand God does not condemn us. He loves us and has already provided our healing and sin sacrifice through Jesus Christ. We need to understand also that we no longer have a sinful nature (Rom. 6:6-14; 2 Cor. 5:21). Christ took care of that on the cross, and then He clothed us in His righteousness. We do, however, have sinful habits that we've learned from being in the world that have to be broken. As we learn and grow in Christ and the word, our minds will be renewed, causing our beliefs to change and our sin habits to be broken. In my journey, I've discovered that I have to continually give those habits over to God and allow Him to help me to overcome them. It's no different than when we first came to Christ. We knew that there was nothing that we could do to save ourselves, and that is why we needed a Savior. We still need Him in this journey. God tells us in His word that He is transforming us into His image from glory to glory (2 Cor. 3:18).

Investing in yourself is another important step. You can't do it alone. It's okay to ask for help. You are not an island unto yourself. Ask God to lead you to the right people and resources. He will do it.

As part of our identity in Christ, we all have a calling on our lives. My calling was revealed to me years ago and receiving it was quite a challenge. You see, I had difficulty seeing myself fulfilling the role of evangelist. It wasn't anything I would have ever chosen for myself. It came at a time when I wasn't quite sure of who I was, and believe it or not I was clueless about that fact as well. After several years of being a backslider, God saw fit to place godly women in my life who ministered to me at a point and time that I really needed it. And because of their ministry to me, I decided to rededicate my life to serving the Lord. I joined Macedonia Baptist Church on October 4, 1992. Shortly after rededicating my life to the Lord, one of the ladies that ministered to me was led to attend an evangelism class being offered at New Mount Olive Baptist Church and she told me that God had placed on her heart to invite me to join this class. I joined the class and went through the evangelism training and completed the training on September 7, 1993. I didn't understand at the time what was going on in my life and I had never even thought about there being any special purpose for my existence.

Time went by and I hadn't thought much about the evangelism training, at least not in the sense of seeking a calling, until I heard my friend talking about her ministry to a young lady who was waiting on a heart transplant and she called herself an evangelist. I began to wonder what the purpose was for my going through the evangelism training, was that my calling? Was that the purpose? I asked myself. I had heard that every person has some calling or purpose for existing and I began to ask God if that was my calling.

Is that why I went through the evangelism training? I said "Lord God is this what I am? Am I supposed to use this title? I don't understand Lord, is this what I am supposed to do? Is this how you want to use me? If it is Lord, then you're going to have to reveal it to me. The Lord began leading me to Ephesians 4:11-12 and 2 Timothy 4:5 and I would read these passages over and over. This to me was one sign of confirmation but I needed more.

One Sunday morning I went to Church and a young man named Justin, who was a member of Macedonia at the time, came forward and announced his call to preach the gospel and I sat there on the pew and I said to the Lord, “Lord see, I’ve always seen people come forward to announce their call to preach, but I’ve never seen anyone come forward to announce their call to be an evangelist. If this is my calling, I wouldn’t know what to do. Sometime later, not exactly sure how much time had passed, it was on another Sunday morning and I was getting ready for Church. I dressed the kids and finished up a few things. I went back to the room to get the kids and they had gotten into some paint. The paint was everywhere, on their clothes, on the carpet, on the sheets, and the mattress. Any other time I would have gotten so upset and frustrated I would have changed my mind about going to Church but all of a sudden, I remembered a sermon that Bishop Courtney McBeth, Calvary Revival Church, had preached a few years earlier while I was watching his ministry on television, about how Satan will use your circumstances to make you miss out on your blessing. I knew at that moment that something was going to happen at Church that I needed to see. I told the devil that his tactics were not going to work and I got the kids cleaned up. I cleaned up as much paint as I could out of the carpet and off of the mattress, and threw the sheets in the wash. I went to church that morning and when I walked in Rev. Regina Contrares was waiting at the door and approached me and told me that the Lord had told her to tell me to take the kids to the nursery because there was something He wanted me to see that morning. I did as I was told and took the kids to the nursery. I sat in the same spot on the same pew that I had sat on the day that Justin had announced his call to preach and that morning Mrs. Mary Lumpkins went forward and announced her call to be an outreach evangelist. As if God was speaking directly in my ear, God said to me, “remember the day that you sat right here in this same spot and Justin went forward to announce his call to preach and you told me that you had always seen people come forward to announce their call to preach but you had never seen anyone announce their call to be an evangelist and you wouldn’t know what to do, well this is what you do.... I said “oh my God!” Well, that week, my pastor, Rev. Alfred A. Terrell was in revival so I couldn't get in contact with him, but I felt that the Lord was telling me to wait until after the retreat. I had a women's retreat the following weekend so I waited. As we were getting settled in for our first day of the retreat the speaker asked who was responsible for inviting her to speak and she looked at me and said, stop questioning if you are called. You are called. On the second day of the retreat the speaker spoke on spiritual gifts and she opened her Bible and began to read Ephesians 4:11. I recognized that God had revealed to me what my calling was and confirmed it in my spirit and there was no doubt that God had called me to the office of evangelist. As God gave me confirmation after confirmation, I chose to blindly accept the call on my life, not knowing what I was agreeing to. I just knew that it was something that I had to do. That Sunday after returning from the retreat I spoke with my pastor. When I approached my pastor to let Him know all that I had been going through as it related to me discovering my calling, he told me that he already knew and that he was just waiting on me.

The following Sunday, May 12, 1996, Mother's Day, I announced my call to be an evangelist. I preached my initial sermon and was licensed on February 9, 1997. I was ordained on October 10, 1999.

God wants to reveal so much to us about who we are, but we have to slow down and pay attention to the things that are happening in our lives and ask God questions. I promise you that if you ask, He will answer. It may not come at the time that you expect it to come nor in the way that you desire it to come but your answer will come. You just have to believe it and expect it.

It's time that our eyes are opened to the reality that, that which we have heard, seen, lived, learned, and believed while growing up in this world has blinded us and kept us from discovering who we truly are and walking in the fullness of who we are as kingdom citizens.

Our values and our beliefs were all shaped by our upbringing, the environment that we grew up in, the people we hung around with, and the so-called social norms, religious views, political views, and other people's perceptions of us, etc. We allowed others to choose for us what our lives are supposed to look like, what was acceptable or unacceptable for us based on laws and rules that were created by people who were no better than anyone else in this world. Now don't get me wrong, laws and rules are needed and we should follow them as long as they don't fall outside of the will of God.

If you have been searching for meaning and purpose in life, if you have struggled with figuring out who you are and why you exist in the world, I believe this book is for you. I believe that we were all created with a purpose in mind (Jer. 29:11, Col. 1:16). We are not just here to exist, work, have fun, pay bills and someday die. We have assignments to fulfill for a greater cause than ourselves and seeking God, doing that internal work, and allowing God to transform us into who He has created us to be is where we need to start if we are ever going to fulfill it.

Get ready to walk out of the shackles that have held you bound. Lies are about to be revealed and annihilated. Religious mindsets and facades are about to be torn down. Strongholds are about to be demolished and you are about to discover who you truly are and fall head over heels in love with God and the person that God created you to be.

3

MISTAKEN IDENTITY

Identity is that which makes you, you. Your make-up, character, personality, and individuality. Identity is an inward thing not based on factors outside of us, although outside factors play a role in shaping us and our views on life. We, however, allow outside factors to define who we are instead of allowing God to define us. After all, He is the one that created us.

When someone asks, "Tell me who you are?" we usually describe ourselves according to what we do. We have become accustomed to identifying ourselves based on our roles in society. We are not accustomed to separating our who from our do.

Throughout our lives, we go through stages of transition and growth. We experience lots of things that shape us and define who we come to believe that we are. We identify ourselves as a daughter, cousin, friend, sister, brother, wife, husband, mother, father, doctor, lawyer, case manager, or whatever our career title is. We also allow other people to define who we are, which includes what media i.e., television, radio, magazines, social media, etc., has portrayed as normal, acceptable, unacceptable, and politically correct and we take ownership of it. The trouble with that is these things can change and most assuredly always do. When they do, we are left wondering once again "who am I." The rate of change in these external factors happens pretty much daily. Sometimes on a moment-by-moment basis.

So, when we allow the world to dictate who we are the very foundation of our identity is shaken and we scramble to redefine ourselves in something or someone else every time one of those factors changes. When we accept and embrace the opinions of others about who they believe we are, we lose the essence of who we truly are.

Like so many others, I thought I knew me. I thought I was so in tune with who I was until the day that my life took a drastic turn and came crashing down around me. That is when I discovered that I didn't know myself as well as I thought. Nor did I know God as well as I thought I did. I had never taken the time to get to know myself, let alone learn to love me. I was so broken and so lost and didn't know where to turn. I hit rock bottom.

As a child, I went through life pretty much, going through the motions and mimicking what I saw, identifying myself with who others perceived and told me I was. What others said about me became what I perceived myself to be. They were not always nice things, and therefore it caused me to have such low self-esteem. I had little self-confidence, and I didn't value myself. You see we don't understand that our words have power. "Death and life are in the power of the tongue…" (ESV, Proverbs 18:21). I had a teacher in 3rd grade that would tell me that I smelled bad. People would tell me that I was stupid. I didn't get very good grades in school so I believed them. I was told by my mom that I was just like my dad; he wasn't anything and I wasn't going to be anything either. As a child this was devastating. I didn't understand why she felt that way. When I got older, I learned that it wasn't that she hated me but because I looked like my dad, I reminded her of him and she was still dealing with the pain of their divorce. I was the most accessible target. I carried that rejection for a long time. Eventually, I matured, I learned that I had to forgive and I did. I'm not bashing my mom. I love my parents and have a good relationship with them and I am very much a daddy's girl. I share that to let you know that it was words like these that caused me to have such low self-esteem and such a poor self-image. We say things not realizing the scars that they are causing. Be careful how you talk to people. Parent be mindful of how you speak to your children. Build each other up instead of tearing each other down.

All the things I had been through in my life were being played out over and over again daily. The saddest part is that I didn't realize this until very late in life. I didn't understand that all of what I had been through was being recorded in my subconscious mind and was shaping the way I thought and believed about myself and the world around me and would ultimately be the lens through which all of my decisions in life would be made.

I'm pulling back the curtains on this to reveal the lies that we so readily believe because we accept them as the norm. We desensitize ourselves to the ills in the world because we get used to it, we allow it and fail to stand up against it. We say this is just how the world is. This is just how it's going to be and the reality is, that couldn't be further from the truth.

If we allow it to continue to go on, we pass down those lies to our children and their children for generations to come. It's a poison that is slowly killing us and we have to start now to change it. This book is one of the steps I'm taking to create that change.

Allow me to give you an example of what happens when your identity is found in something or someone other than God. This was my rock bottom.

You see, I was happily married and had a beautiful family. I had no idea that my husband did not feel the same. Yes, we had our ups and downs, every marriage does but I loved my husband. He was everything to me. I won't go into details, but he decided that he no longer wanted to be married. His goals in life did not include me. So, we separated and divorced. I was devastated. My family, my identity, and my life as I knew it was being stripped away.

I had mistakenly, as most women so often unknowingly do, misplaced my identity or created an identity in what it was that I did. My role as wife and mother became my identity. Now that my family was falling apart, I began to question who I was. I had no identity apart from that. I discovered that I didn't know what I liked, what I enjoyed doing, nor how to be alone and be content and comfortable with me. I had no real identity going into marriage so when it ended, I was back to square one.

I was so devastated by what was going on in my life that I even contemplated suicide. Yes, I did. I took a bottle of pills from my nightstand and poured them into my hand. I was getting ready to take them and I would have, had it not been for my relationship with God.

Although I found out as I continued my journey that I didn't know Him as well as I thought I knew Him but, I thank God, I knew Him well enough to recognize His voice. God knew exactly how to get my attention. As I sat there listening to the voice in my head saying things like "go ahead take them, he'll be sorry once you're gone." "He'll regret walking away and wish you were still here." "Go ahead, take them, you'll be better off." "You know you can't tell anybody about this because you are a minister and you'll be talked about and judged." I listened to the lies of the enemy intently agreeing with them until another voice stepped in. This voice I recognized as the voice of God. He said, "What are you doing? You are the one that is always telling everyone that there is nothing in this world so bad that it is worth taking your own life, yet you sit here with this bottle of pills in your hand. What are you doing?" I knew it was God. He continued, "The world is going to go on whether you are in it or not. What are you going to do?"

At that moment I put the pills back in the bottle. With tears in my eyes, I cried out to God for help. I took the bottle of pills and sat them on the nightstand by my bed. I knew that I was weak and I didn't want the pills to be tempting again so I took the bottle of pills and flushed them down the toilet so that I wouldn't be tempted anymore. I went to talk to my husband and told him what I was about to do and told him that I needed to call someone because I needed help. He told me to call whoever I needed to call. I called my pastor and she came over and ministered to me. The support I received showed Gods' amazing love for me.

As I continued my journey through the grieving process of losing my marriage, I found myself making bad decisions after bad decisions. I felt worthless, less than a woman because my husband didn't want me. I was speaking negative things about myself, calling myself names, telling myself that I'm not desirable as a woman, no one else will want me either. I felt empty, ugly, and unlovable. I just wanted to be loved. It was because my husband wanted me that made me feel valued in the first place. Now the value was gone. The fact that he wanted me meant that I was special, I mattered to someone. Maybe I wasn't as ugly as people had been saying I was or that I believed I was. Having his children gave me even more of a sense of being needed and valued, more of an identity. These thoughts were making me crazy. I felt as though I was losing my mind. Who am I? Why am I here? Why is all of this happening to me?

I just wanted someone to love me and to show me that I was desirable as a woman. I went from one sexual encounter to another, even joining online dating sites because I was desperate. I did not want to be alone. But alone was where God had me. I didn't understand it at the time, and I would question God because even being in those encounters with those men left me still lonely and alone. I was still empty.

Some nights I would scream out hysterically in agony. I would curl up on my floor in a fetal position, cry and condemn myself and repent over and over again and tell God I was not going to do it again, only to do it again. I was sure that God was angry with me. I went to church on Sundays. I spent a lot of time at the altar because I was tormented by the lie I was living, but I didn't know how to stop it. I begged God to help me. I begged God to sit me down (from my position as evangelist) because I knew my life was not conducive to serving in the capacity of an evangelist, and I didn't want to be transferring anything to anyone (spiritually speaking).

I couldn't tell anyone what I was doing because I was so ashamed and the words the enemy spoke to me when I was about to commit suicide still rang in my ears. "You can't tell anybody. You'll be judged and condemned."

The guilt and shame from those sexual encounters were weighing heavy on me. I hated myself even more because of what I was doing. I lived in constant fear that someone would find out and I would be judged and condemned.

With each encounter or relationship, I entered into, I would set the boundary, no sex outside of marriage but would ultimately cross that boundary because I was made to feel desirable. Again, going home each time feeling so worthless for going against my values.

I suffered from depression and anxiety of the worst kind. I functioned most every day because I had to. I had bills to pay and children to take care of so I went to work. I would put on my mask and go do what I had to do. At the end of the day, I would go home and bask in my pity party only to start the cycle all over again.

Remember I told you earlier that alone was where God had me? There were some things that God desired to do in me and in my life, which required my isolation. It was during this season in my life that God began to develop in me who I am. This season would begin my journey of healing and finding out my true identity in Christ.

I thank God for the three Christian sister-friends He had placed in my life. I could share with them what I was going through and knew I would not be judged. They prayed for me, they encouraged me and they were there for me when I needed to talk. I also had a friend who was an older gentleman. He happened to be a social worker and he believed that my husband and I would get back together. It seemed that he always knew when I would be sitting at home alone in the dark, wallowing in self-pity and allowing myself to become depressed and anxious. He would call and invite me out for breakfast, to go bowling, or to shoot pool, depending on what time of the day it was. He would minister to me and allow me to share my pain. I shared very little. He would tell me that I had to learn how to love myself and if that meant standing in front of a mirror buck naked until I fell in love with every single flaw that I had, then I needed to do that. He would say if I didn't love myself then I would not be able to love anyone else. I took that to heart and I began learning how to love myself. It wasn't easy. It was uncomfortable going out alone, spending time with myself. The silence was awkward. I would force myself because I knew it was necessary. Little by little I began to be comfortable with myself, by spending time alone and learning to love myself. It wasn't until I fell in love with every single part of myself that I began to come up out of that place of depression, anxiety, and self-sabotage.

I needed to be in the season of aloneness. I didn't like it but I discovered that without it, I would not have learned my true identity in Christ nor how to truly love myself. In learning how to love myself, I was able to forgive and to genuinely love others, including my ex-husband. It was rough there for a while but we were able to work through and overcome all of the things we had gone through and become friends again. So, no matter what season you may find yourself in at this very moment take a moment to ask yourself if you are living a mistaken identity? Have you allowed other people to dictate to you who you are? Truth is that no one knows who you are, not even you. We have not yet become who we are becoming. We are who He has created us to be, and He is continually working in us, transforming us into His image from glory to glory. We mistakenly assume who we believe someone is by their actions or where they currently are in their journey in life. The only one that knows who we are is God. He knows exactly who He created us to be. This is why we need to stay connected to Him. If you feel like you are in a season of aloneness then ask God where He is in all of it. What is it that He wants to do in, to and through you in this season? What is it that you have to learn in this season?

Take the time to get to know God, take the time to get to know you, be comfortable with you, and truly love you unconditionally. (This is very good practice in any season). Your season of aloneness doesn't have to be as crazy as mine was. God loves you and He is right there with you no matter what season you find yourself in. Take the time to look for Him. I believe you will find Him. He says in Jeremiah 29:13 *"And you will seek Me and find Me when you search for Me with all your heart."* I was able to look back and see where He was in all of what I went through. He never left me nor forsook me. He remained faithful to His word. He was waiting on me to seek Him, not other people, for what I needed. When I did, He helped me through the process.

If you can relate to my story, know and understand that you have the power to change your life. Make a choice today to develop a relationship with God and start your journey to find your true identity in Christ. Making that identity shift starts and ends with going to your Creator, who is God. Allow Him to tell you exactly who you are and to work in you and transform you into who He created you to be. Allow Him to be who He desires to be for you. When you do that, you will find that He is exactly what you need whatever the need may be. Take a moment right now to reflect on what season you may be in right now. Then ask God who or what He desires to be for you at this very moment. Now write it down.

4

STEPPING OUT OF YOUR COMFORT ZONE

I was not the brightest kid in school. I struggled through most of my classes bringing home report cards with mostly C's, D's, and F's. Except for English and Government, my favorite subjects, I managed to bring home some A's and B's in those classes. My grades were so bad I failed the 10th grade and had to repeat that year. I was upset, but it didn't bother me, not too much anyway, because my brother was a year behind me, and we ended up graduating together, and besides that, I learned more the second time around. Besides the challenges of academics, I was not very popular in school, and remember I shared that I struggled with low self-esteem most of my life, always trying to fit in and feeling like I never measured up.

I became pregnant during my last year in high school and never even thought about going to university. I mean what university would take me with a GPA that was probably so low it was laughable. I was afraid to even find out what my GPA was. To this day I still don't know. I had my baby a month after graduating and went on to eventually get a job.

My daughter was going on 7 years old when I married her father. We had two more children and I worked full time outside of the home. When my oldest daughter was in middle school, she began attending a program called "Educational Talent Search" (ETS) offered through Hampton University. It was and is a program that encourages and prepares young people to complete high school and go on to post-secondary education. The experience my daughter and I had in that program spiked a desire in me to want to go to college. But how could I? After all, I was now in my 30's. I was also a wife and mother of three, two of them in elementary school and I worked full time. I had no idea what kind of career I wanted to pursue but I had a job and that was all the ambition I had at the time.

My desire to go to university continued to grow. Although it was a scary decision to make, after spending lots of time in prayer, I decided to take a chance. I stepped out of my comfort zone and went to talk to my daughter's counselor at ETS to find out what I needed to do to go to university. Her counselor not only provided me with the information I needed to make an informed decision and to choose a school to pursue; she also went with me to the school. She sat down with me, and held my hand through the process of asking questions and finally registering. Yes, I registered. I took full-time classes and worked hard to pass each class. I had recently been licensed into the ministry as an evangelist and I wanted to enhance my ministry so I chose Religion as my major. After being there for a while I felt as though God was leading me to add Sociology as a second major. I had no idea what I would do with it but out of obedience, I did it.

Math was my most challenging subject. You see I never went beyond basic math in high school. I had the mentality that I would only take what I needed to get by. A placement test indicated that I take a pre-algebra class to get me to the place where I was ready to take algebra classes for credit. I enlisted my oldest daughter and a couple of high school students from my church to tutor me through my math journey. I was carrying a 4.0 GPA and was very proud of myself. I failed the first algebra class that I took for credit. My GPA dropped drastically. I had to take the algebra class again. I passed it but it took a while to bring my GPA back up.

My oldest daughter and I marched in the summer of 2002. She graduated from high school and I graduated from university with a double major and honors with a 3.8 GPA.

I have to say the struggle was real. I spent a lot of time in prayer throughout my university years and by the grace of God, I made it. The most amazing thing that I discovered was that God already had my career lined up. He had opened up doors for me that I had no idea would lead to a career that I grew to love, working with individuals with intellectual and developmental disabilities.

As I reminisced about my life's journey up to that point, I saw how God had provided the two years of case management experience I needed to move me into that career. I was able to volunteer as a Court Appointed Special Advocate for the Juvenile Court System during my time in university. The program allowed me to register the day before the training was to start.

Originally, I was told that everyone had already been sworn in and that it was too late for this round of training but I could sign up for the next round of training. I continued to push for that training session because I felt like God was saying this was my time. I explained that there was not going to be an issue with the background check because I was currently working in a position in which one was required. After putting me on hold for a few moments the lady came back to the phone and told me that they normally wouldn't do this but they decided to let me attend the training starting the next day. I had to go down to the courthouse, complete the application, and be sworn in that afternoon. I did that, started, and completed the training. There were so many other things that God revealed to me during that time. Had I not gotten that two years of case management experience I would not have qualified for the very first position that launched my career. God had a plan for my life.

When I decided to step out of my comfort zone and trust Him, He showed me the path to something I never imagined for myself.

No matter the challenges you've faced in life up to this point, whether you became a teen parent like me or grew up poor, came from a broken home, were in an abusive relationship, or faced some other difficult challenge in life and you had no hope of ever becoming anything or ever achieving your dreams, I want to encourage you to not give up. Life does not end at that point in your life. God has a plan for your life and it is amazing. You can dream, you can achieve, and you can have a life more incredible than you ever thought possible if you are determined, remain persistent, persevere through the tough times, and allow God to guide you. You will probably get lots of "noes" as you press forward but keep pressing forward anyway and looking for your "yes". It is out there and all you need is one "yes" to get you to where you and God desire you to be. It happened for me many times, it can happen for you as well.

5

NO IDENTITY OF HER OWN

I meet people all of the time whose identities are tied to the people in their lives. Most of them don't realize it, nor do they realize how it is affecting the people that are connected to them. This is the story of a woman whose identity was totally tied to her adult child and her role as mother.

Listening to her response each time I spoke with her about her adult child's desire to move to another home always grieved me. The low self-esteem, and the lack of self-identity was very familiar and I recognized it immediately. I could imagine all of the negative things she was saying to herself because I had been there before, repeating the words, I'm worthless, I'm nothing, I don't matter, I'm a failure, I'll never amount to anything to herself on a daily basis. Being familiar with the spirit of depression and anxiety I could discern that she too was being plagued with the same spirit. You see her adult child has several disabilities and she is the legal guardian because the adult child is not able to make informed decisions. She could not let her adult child go, not because of the disabilities, but because her identity was tied up in her child. Her response to her child's request to move was always what will I do if my child moves? Who will I be then? She would not allow herself to see things from her child's point of view or anyone else's for that matter. She was the mother and if she allowed her child to move then she would be nothing. She would be lost. She would not be needed anymore. This was her mindset.

The adult child was angry and bitter because as an adult watching as all of the other sibling move away and not be able to do the same was heartbreaking. This individual interacts with other adult peers with disabilities who have been able to leave home and yet this individual felt stuck. The adult child would strike out in violence against the guardian because their voice was not heard.

The family was falling apart because she had no regard for the feelings or desires of anyone else in the home. She would say, if I let my child go, I won't have anything. My child needs me. If I let my child go, I won't feel needed anymore.

I took a chance at initiating what I felt was a much-needed conversation with her. Initially sharing how I hoped I was not crossing any boundaries. I started by acknowledging her feelings and then sharing the heart of her adult child and their need to be heard, as the adult child had shared with me on several occasions, pointing out also that as an adult the individual deserves the chance to grow and mature. She listened intently and acknowledged that I was right but that it was hard for her.

Going where I felt the Spirit of God leading me, I began to address the low self-esteem, the depression and anxiety, the lack of self-worth, her poor self-concept and how her view of herself was affecting not only her but her entire household. I began to recite the words that I could imagine her saying to herself. The tears began to flow. She said that I was so on point. She wondered how I knew all of the things she was going through and all of the things she was saying to herself. This allowed me to share my story, letting her know that I had been there. I had said some of those words to myself. I had suffered with depression and anxiety. I had even contemplated suicide but God healed and delivered me from all of that and that is why I am so passionate about women realizing their true value and identity.

Acknowledging her Christianity and how as a Sunday school teacher, believing what she is teaching is necessary. I suggested that she really study and meditate on the word of God and what He says about who she is in Him. I also suggested that she take some time to really do some deep self-discovery because she is not going to find what she is looking for in other people. It all starts with looking within and embracing and loving all that she is. Holding onto her adult child so tightly is not going to fix what's going on inside of her. As I began to encourage her with words of comfort and empowering words of who she really is in Christ verses who she believes she is, it started to break through some of the lies that she was believing about herself.

She continued to cry. I again apologized if I was crossing any boundaries. I suggested that she do an exercise based on a question that God asked me to consider. He said if you take away everything that you've identified with, being wife, mother, employer, employee, entrepreneur, grandmother, etc. all of those things that are outside of you who would you be? I asked her to sit down and really think hard about that question and write down who she is if all of the external self-identifiers were nonexistent. Why don't you take a moment right now to do that as well?

____

____

____

____

____

____

She listened intently as I encouraged her and as I advocated for her adult child's needs and desires. She shared how she realizes that it's all her and she is holding her child back. She stated that she would consider all that I had said. She thanked me and said that our talk was exactly what she needed. I encouraged her to take it one day at a time. It's a journey and conquering the lies and beliefs are not going to happen overnight. As she conquers one, more will surface. So, learning how to take those negative thoughts and beliefs and replace them with more positive ones is how she should start. Begin studying and meditating on the scriptures, especially identity scriptures and write them out and rehearse them several times a day, post them where she can see them so that she can be reminded until she begins to believe what God says about her, spend time in God's presence and ask the Holy Spirit to give her proper interpretation of the scriptures.

All of these things should help her and she should start seeing some transformation as the word of God begins to take root and grow.

It's important to realize that how you feel about yourself not only affects you, but also affects other people. If you don't love or value yourself then you won't be able to love or value others. You can't give what you don't have. Seeking your value and validation from others and having the need to be needed will never bring you real satisfaction. It will never fill the void in your life or bring the healing that you need. Seeking the Father and allowing Him to be all that you need and to do the work that needs to be done in you will fill the void, bring the healing and deliverance you need, and change your life.

6

YOU MUST KNOW WHO YOU ARE

When God created you, He created you with an already established identity. The person you are yet to become is already inside of you. Two scriptures that confirm that fact are:

> ESV, Gen. 1:27 "*So God created man in His image; in the image of God he created him; male and female he created them.*" And NKJV, Psalm 139:14-17 "*I will praise You, for I am fearfully and wonderfully made; Marvelous are Your works, And that my soul knows very well. My frame was not hidden from You, When I was made in secret, And skillfully wrought in the lowest parts of the earth. Your eyes saw my substance, being yet unformed. And in Your book they all were written, The days fashioned for me, When as yet there were none of them. How precious also are Your thoughts to me, O God! How great is the sum of them!*"

In previous chapters, I've shared why it is dangerous to base our identity on what someone else has said to us or about us. People in society like labels. Labels can be dangerous though because we become so attached to them that we wear them like a badge of honor even to the destruction of our dreams and our lives. By allowing society to dictate our identity we end up getting our feelings hurt and going through unnecessary pain and rejection because we have embraced all of those lies and created these mistaken identities. These identities cause us to become depressed, and live hopeless, helpless lives with no motivation and no vision. They cause us to live below our potential in life and in Christ because we don't value who we are or what we have to offer. It can also have a reverse effect. It can cause pride to build up in us to where we think we are all of that and we judge and condemn others. We become boastful and live a life that lacks integrity and good character.

Seeking our identity in people, things, positions, and possessions will always leave us feeling empty and unfulfilled. That is because we're trying to find what we think we need in these other resources when that desire for something greater than ourselves was put there by the Great Creator (God) as a desire for Him. This is why finding our identity in Christ is essential.

In the previous chapter, I referred to a question God asked me while I was writing this book. He asked me to consider this, "if everything outside of me that I have identified myself with was stripped away, who would I be?" The memory of my ex-husband asking me for divorce and saying that he didn't love me anymore came flooding back. That was the point in my life when I realized that I didn't know who I was. Yes, I had lived a lifetime with low self-esteem, people-pleasing, and looking for validation and approval from others, but even in all of that it never really hit me until that moment that my identity was wrapped up in who I was connected to. It was that question that caused me to realize how far I had come and to finally be able to lay to rest the identity of my past and to truly take hold of the identity that I have in Christ.

Now I know who I am apart from anything on the outside of me. God is still teaching me and I will continually be learning all of what my identity in Him entails until the day He calls me home.

It is so important that you learn who you truly are also. Knowing this vital information brings life and hope, purpose, and peace.

When God created us in the beginning, He did not just speak us into existence. He put His hands on us. He molded us. He shaped us. This is found in Genesis 2:7, 22. That means that we are special and we mean something. We have value. We have worth.

When we say we have no worth or value it is because we are believing the lies that people have told us about who we are, the image that society paints as acceptable and politically correct. They tell us that we will never be anything and we'll never amount to anything and we believe them. We begin to speak it over ourselves and they become self-fulling prophecies.

We will never know who we are and we will never find the satisfaction and fulfillment that our soul and spirit desires until we go to the one that created us and asks Him who we are and what our purpose in life is. If we never do that, we will continue to live our lives in defeat. We will continue to live our lives with no hope and no direction. We will continue to allow circumstances, situations, actions, inaction, and opinions of people to control us. Understand, victory in this life is only possible in and through Christ. We need to understand that that deep longing and desire that we have on the inside of us was put there by God for Him and Him alone. It is through covenant with Him that that desire will be satisfied and fulfilled. We are never alone when we are in Christ because He never leaves us nor forsakes us. We can count on Him to be constant in our lives.

So, if we don't build a relationship with Him, we will never know who we are. We will never know our full potential, let alone reach it. We have to stay connected to the source of our identity. James 1:17-18 tells us that, "*Every good gift and every perfect gift is from above, coming down from the Father of lights, with whom there is no variation or shadow due to change. Of his own will, he brought us forth by the word of truth, that we should be a kind of first fruits of his creatures.*" We are good and perfect gifts. We came from God. He created us and He said everything that He created was good. You need to know today, THAT YOU ARE GOOD. There is nothing wrong with you. We have been taught wrong, we've listened to the wrong people, we've learned wrong, we've allowed wrong things to be sewn into us and so we have to unlearn and re-learn. We have to learn what truth is, what God's truth is.

We belong to God. We were created in His image and likeness. We have to get our minds wrapped around that fact. We are here. We are not a mistake. We have an identity in Him that is constant and unchanging and we have a purpose. We are God's masterpiece and we are fearfully and wonderfully made (Eph. 2:10; Ps. 139:14).

Just like any product that is made, when a person starts to create that product in his mind, he creates it with an identity and with a specific purpose in mind, he can tell us what that product is (identity) and its purpose. Likewise, God created us, He is the only one that can tell us who we are and the purpose we are meant to serve. So that is why we must go to God our Father and ask Him so that we can know our true identity. We don't want to just live and let life happen. I did that for far too long.

We all were created on purpose, with purpose, and for purpose. Your identity is tied to that purpose. You have an assignment to fulfill while you are here in the earth and you won't find it until you discover who you are. You won't know who you are unless you ask the one that created you. Have you done that yet? If not, you can take a moment and do that right now. He wants you to know and He will tell you. Once you get the answer that's when life truly begins to have meaning for you. That's when vision for life starts to unfold. That's when life starts to happen.

It is God who transforms us. He will bring the change that needs to happen in us. We don't have to struggle to change ourselves and get frustrated because we keep falling short and falling back into some of the things we use to do. We just have to be willing to allow Him to do the work that He desires to do in us. 2 Corinthians 3:18 says, "*And we all, with unveiled face, beholding the glory of the Lord, are being transformed into the same image from one degree of glory to another. For this comes from the Lord who is the Spirit.*" As we keep our eyes on Him, as we read and study

His word, as we spend quality time with Him building intimacy with Him, He is transforming us into His image from glory to glory. He works from the inside out.

The word of God is a mirror to us, and as we allow our minds to be transformed by the word of God then our behaviors and actions will follow. We have to allow God to transform us into the image that He created us in. He is not interested in fixing the old us. That person died when we accepted Christ as our Lord and our Savior. He wants us to enter the newness of life, to become the person He created us to be, to embrace our new identity in Him and to embrace our new home, the kingdom of God. That is why the transformation. It's a transition that we have to make.

> *"Therefore, if anyone is in Christ, he is a new creation; old things have passed away; behold, all things have become new"* (NKJV, 2 Cor. 5:17) *"and [He] raised us up together, and made us sit together in the heavenly places in Christ Jesus, ..."* (NKJV, Eph. 2:6).

It's important to know and understand that we do not just exist in the world without reason. We are to do something great in the world. We were created to bring glory to God. We have a calling, assignments, the anointing, gifts, talents, and the ability to complete it (2 Peter 1:3). This is true for every one of us.

God desires that we have and enjoy life. That can't happen until you are sure of who you are. You have to be secure in your identity because if you are not, life and Satan will continue to knock you down and wreak havoc in your life, keep you distracted and confused so that you can't have and enjoy all that God desires for you to have and enjoy. Victory is ours in Christ. Your identity in Him is tied to victory. He calls you His son/daughter, an heir and joint heir with Jesus Christ, kings and priests, and His masterpiece. This is your true identity and none of those factors we addressed previously that change with the wind can alter your identity in Christ.

State of the County Luncheon
March 9, 2022

Welcome — President Marty Sauls, Jasper County Chamber of Commerce

Presentation of Colors — Jasper County Color Guard

Invocation — Councilman Tommy Rhodes, Town of Ridgeland

Introduction of Guests — Marty Sauls

Speakers

- Mayor Joey Malphrus, Town of Ridgeland
- Mayor Harry Williams, City of Hardeeville
- Chairwoman, Barbara Clark, Jasper County Council

Introduction of Guest Speaker — Marty Sauls

Guest Speaker — The Honorable Mark Hammond, South Carolina Secretary of State

Closing Remarks — Marty Sauls

7

TRUSTING HIM IN THE PREPARATION SEASON

During my season of aloneness, I would pray to God to send me my husband so that I could stop giving myself away. But I was still trying to make it happen for myself. I was looking and having these encounters because I was not doing it in God's way. Had I not gone through this season of aloneness and preparation I would have probably gone into another marriage with the same mistaken identity and probably would have ended up in the same predicament again. I had to discover my true identity in Christ and learn to love me so that I could love the man that God had for me. God had to perform internal surgery on me. Some chronic identity issues were going on inside of me that only He could heal, some broken places that needed repairing that only He could repair. Once I started listening to Him and decided to do it His way that is when things started changing. When I was on the road to recovery, and my mindset had shifted, then and only then did He open my eyes to see and receive what I had been praying for and what He had prepared for me.

The last thing I asked God to do for me so that I could recognize my husband when he sent him, was to have him set the no sex outside of the marriage boundary because I was tired of setting the boundary and crossing it. The sad thing in all my craziness during this season is that I knew that no matter who I was attracted to if I had sex with him, he was not my husband.

You see, God had told me in my quiet time with Him that anyone I had sex with was not my husband. Did you catch that revelation? God knew that I was going to have sexual encounters outside of marriage. I missed that revelation. That was a rhema word specifically, for me. God was not surprised by those encounters. Yet I beat myself up for years because I was disappointing myself and I believed that God was mad at me. I told you I didn't know God as well as I thought I did. I learned that God is so loving and truly enduring. He wants to protect us so He provides us with His word and His Holy Spirit. He gives us instruction for life through His word but when we read all of the thou shalt nots and warnings, we think God is trying to keep us from having fun and enjoying life when in actuality they protect us from so many unseen dangers, circumstances and situations that could happen in our lives if we would only take heed. I could have saved myself a lot of heartaches if I had heeded the word and His instructions.

I thought I had found the man I wanted to be my husband until I crossed that boundary with him. I knew he wasn't but I fell head over heels for him and I wanted him to be the one. We dated off and on for about two years before it finally ended. Shortly after, I discovered that God had already sent my husband but I didn't recognize him because he didn't come in the package that I was looking for. (How often do we miss what God has for us because we already have in mind how we want God to answer?) We were introduced by a mutual friend and were familiar with each other but had not spoken except to say hi if we saw each other. He would open doors for me and I would say thank you, look the other way and keep it moving. I knew he was interested in me but I was not interested in him in the slightest.

I had prayed for tall dark and handsome. I had my laundry list of what I wanted and I had presented it to God. In my prayer time, however, I also said, "yet not my will but your will God, I want what you want for me. You know what's best for me."

The person that God sent for me I avoided like a plague. I ran from him for almost a year, not giving him the time of day. This man knew that I was his wife. He continued to pursue me even though I was not interested in him at all. He shared with me later that he was beginning to question whether he had heard God right because I didn't appear to be the least bit interested in him.

God had to get my attention. He began dropping this man into my spirit. I would find myself thinking about him and asking God why he was dropping this man in my spirit. I was not interested in him. I knew what I had prayed for and he was not it. God said "you are looking at the outward I look at the heart. Open the book and take a look on the inside." Needless to say, I finally gave in and consented to have a conversation with him. During our first telephone call, he prayed and invited the Holy Spirit into the conversation. We talked for four hours. We ended the phone call and shortly after he called back. He said, "oh yeah, I think we need to set some boundaries." I said, okay! He said, first of all, there will be no sex outside of marriage. I again said, okay! He said that's about all I got, you got any you want to add. I said, nope. That about does it. I recognized that God had heard me and I realized that he may be my husband. I still wasn't convinced though. He continued to talk and he said some other things that got my attention. As he spoke, he would say things that I had prayed to God in secret about. One of the things he said was that I was going to have to teach him how to love me.

I had prayed that God would send someone that I could teach how to love me and he would teach me how to love him so that we could love each other the way that we need to be loved. Sounds corny, doesn't it? but that's what I prayed. I could hear God saying to me each time, you use to pray for that. You stopped asking but I am giving you that, and that too. I was becoming more convinced.

We went on our first date, dinner and a movie. We talked and got to know each other better.

He would pray with me and for me as we got to know each other better. Over the next few days and weeks after our first date, God would give more confirmation that this man was my husband. Steven referred to himself as my Boaz while we were dating. No one knew that but the person that introduced us. One of the confirmations came from the pulpit one Sunday morning. The pastor stopped during her sermon and began to say several times, get rid of the bozo and keep the Boaz, get rid of the bozo and keep the Boaz. It had nothing to do with her sermon. I whispered to God, "I hear you, Lord."

One evening Steven and I were talking and we shared some painful moments from our past. We cried as we shared because we were still broken and needed healing in these areas. After I shared, he got down on one knee and held my hands, and started praying for me. At that very moment, something shifted and broke off of me. I could feel healing taking place. I then prayed for him and we were both able to experience healing in those broken places that night. We dated for 30 days total before getting married. We were both convinced that we were who God had chosen for each other. As of the writing of this book, we are approaching eight years of marriage. God taught me in all of this that His ways are not our ways and when we are serious about wanting His will, He will send exactly what we need. You see, although I was looking for tall, dark, and handsome and thought I had found him, God sent me the great white knight (if you haven't guessed, my husband is white). My husband and I still laugh when I say that.

God wants us to trust Him to provide exactly what we need in His timing. He knows the plans He has for us. He has already written our story (Psalm 139:13-16) we just have to desire His story instead of our own and be willing to allow His story to become a reality in our lives. Let Him know you desire His will for your life. Stop trying to make things happen for yourself. Understand that like me, you will probably have to go through a preparation process. You will also have to be open to something different than what you are used to but if you trust Him, He will come through for you. Don't miss it.

My husband was part of God's plan for me. He has been my biggest cheerleader as I continue to pursue my God-given calling, purpose, and assignments in life. He prays for me. He encourages me. He supports me and I do the same for him. It was one of my prayers to God, that He send someone that supports me in pursuing my kingdom purpose and I could do the same thing for him. When you make that identity shift all of the benefits that come along with being in covenant with the Most High God are at your disposal. God knew what was best for me, so He sent Steven into my life.

What are you trying to make happen in your life that may not be God's will or His best for you? What can you do differently so that you can experience God's will for your life?

8

IT'S ALL ABOUT TRANSFORMATION

The love that God has for us is so amazing. He loves us and receives us just as we are. He draws us (John 6:44) and when we respond and go to Him with a pure heart of repentance and receive His gift of salvation, our journey of relationship with Him begins. His love takes us in and begins transforming us into His image (2 Corinthians 3:18). When I tell you that I am a different person today than I was years ago it's an understatement. I used to curse like a sailor and I knew how to be ugly and give as good as I got if somebody came at me wrong. I remember getting in fights because people talked about me and didn't like me. I liked clubbing. My ex-husband was a DJ and belonged to a van club so we traveled to clubs in different cities and states. For years, I didn't think there was anything wrong with that. It was normal. And I'm not saying going to clubs is wrong or that it's wrong for you. That is between you and God. I'm just saying it was not right for me. I remember sitting in my room one day, just thinking about my life and how I had been living. I was being convicted not condemned. I wanted so much to be pleasing to God. I prayed and asked God to take away anything in my life that wasn't pleasing to Him. I didn't like cursing at my kids. I no longer liked the person I was beginning to see that I was. I had a Christian friend who would always tell me that it made her spirit cringe when I used profanity. I didn't understand that at the time. As I read the scriptures and began to let God have His way in my life, I began to notice a change in me. One day I realized that I wasn't cursing any more. My spirit would cringe whenever someone cursed around me. Even watching TV shows with profanity would make my spirit cringe. It did not feel good at all. I realized that God was allowing me to feel what my Christian sister felt when I used that language around her. To this day, my spirit cringes when I hear profanity. I know it's the Holy Spirit in me. I began to feel uncomfortable in certain places and doing some of the things that I used to do, and family members didn't understand and started to feel like I thought I was better than them because I could not participate in some things that I once did. God also took away the desire to go clubbing. I became very mindful of how I carried myself. God was transforming me. I liked the changes I was seeing in me. I liked the person I was becoming. This was the beginning of the manifestation of my identity shift. What had already happened in the spirit after receiving Christ as Lord and Savior of my life was now becoming a reality in the natural realm. As my mindset changed, my beliefs and behaviors started to change.

We tend to believe that we have to have it all together before we come to God, but the truth is, that we can't change anything within ourselves that will bring the kind of lasting change that really matters, that is why we need Christ.

Growing up in this world has conditioned us to think and believe a certain way. When we enter a relationship with God through Jesus Christ the word of God tells us that we become new creations and old things pass away and everything becomes new (2 Cor. 5:17). This means that all that you've known, all that you've done, all that you've experienced in life is old. It doesn't matter anymore, at least not in the sense that it should control your life. Christ made you brand new. He wiped the slate clean and you get to start all over again. Smile, it's a brand-new day.

You are no longer the person you were before you accepted Christ. There has been a shift. There has been a transition. Yes, you still look the same and it may not feel like anything has changed but it has, and just like you had to grow into the person that you once were, you will also have to grow into the person you have just become and are yet becoming.

You don't go from the bottle (babe in Christ) to eating steak (mature in Christ) overnight. There is a process and it starts with renewing the mind. You see God is in the transforming business. He is not trying to fix the old us. That person died with Christ when we gave our lives to Him. He wants to transform us into who He created us to be. We have no idea of the person that we are yet to become. When I was younger, I had no idea that I would become the person that I am today. I stand amazed at the transformation that God has done in me and I eagerly await to meet the person I am yet to become as He continues the good work, He has begun in me (Phil. 1:6).

It's not easy to make the shift but it's very necessary. I know none of us want to relinquish control but to be successful on our journey to becoming the one He created us to be, we have to allow God to have His way in and through us.

Becoming a student of the word of God is also necessary. It is the only way our minds can be renewed (Rom. 12:1-2). It is the only way our faith can grow. *"So then faith comes by hearing and hearing by the word of God"* (NKJV, Romans 10:17). Sitting under good sound doctrine, receiving the baptism of the Holy Spirit, and dialoguing with God are all important in the process of renewing our minds, understanding our true identity, and walking in who He has created us to be.

There is a battle going on to distract us and to take control of our minds. The enemy does not want us to know who we are. He does not want us to understand the word of God. He does not want us to focus on our relationship with God. He wants us to focus on what we see and what we feel, the temporal things. He will lie to us and use whatever is necessary to distract us and get us off course. This is why developing the right mindset is crucial. This is why the word of God is also very crucial. We have to know and understand the tactics of the enemy. *"The thief does not come except to steal, and to kill, and to destroy..."* (NKJV, John 10:10). We have to know and understand who our Father is and the roles that God the Father, God the Son, and God the Holy Spirit play in our lives. I won't go into a lot of detail because it can get very in-depth. For the sake of this book, I just want to share how very important it is to have the right mindset and to understand your identity in Christ so that you will be able to receive the truth about who you are. I want to encourage and inspire you to take responsibility for your spiritual growth and start pursuing it as if your life depends on it because it does.

The word of God is a seed and when that seed is planted, it begins to take root and grow. God does a work on the inside of us and as we grow in Him, it begins to manifest on the outside. Our lives are being transformed as the word of God becomes more and more a part of who we are. Let me take a moment here to talk about how our past experiences affect us going forward. The mind is very powerful. It has the power to drive us to success or to destroy us.

All that we've learned and experienced is important because it has helped to shape us into the people that we have become and I believe that no matter how bad some of our experiences were, God will use those experiences for good. We just have to surrender all of our past experiences, traumas, hurts, and disappointments to Him and allow Him to turn those tragedies into triumphant treasures and victories.

You see, I can say that now because as I relinquish all of my baggage and let God have it, He takes it and gives me a brand-new outlook on life and I am now taking those experiences and sharing my testimony of how God delivered me, healed me, and transformed my life so that others who may be going through the same things or something similar can see that there is hope.

God truly does work all things for our good (Rom. 8:28). We may not see it at the time but eventually, we can look back and trace His goodness in our lives, but it all starts with renewing our minds and getting rid of the lies, those limiting beliefs that we've allowed to control us all these years.

One of the biggest lies that the enemy has the body of Christ believing is that they can't understand the bible. It's too hard. So, what does the body of Christ do? They don't read or study the bible. I want to let you know that it's not hard to understand the bible. It just takes time.

I will explain in a few minutes. But just know this, he, the devil, wants to keep us ignorant of the word of God because he does not want us to know who we are. He does not want us to discover the authority we have over him. He does not want us to discover the tactics he uses nor how to activate the power we have in Christ.

When we look around it's hard to distinguish the body of Christ from the world, isn't it? It's because many in the body of Christ don't truly understand their true identity. They don't know who they are. They don't understand the power of covenant, specifically the covenant God has with us as His children and the covenant we now have with Him as our Father. They don't understand that there was a shift, a transition from the world to the kingdom of God when we gave our lives to Christ. How do I know this, you ask? Because that was me. I did not understand, but now I do and I am studying and learning so that I can understand better. We need to make the mindset shift that is necessary for us to become who God says we are, the new creation that we became when we chose to accept Jesus Christ as Lord and Savior of our lives. We are still living under the old while expecting to experience the new, but to fully embrace and experience the new we must relinquish the old.

Don't allow the enemy to keep you distracted any longer. Don't allow him to keep you focused on your situation and circumstances. Don't allow him to continue to lie to you and keep you in bondage to your past. He wants to keep you in that place so that you don't fulfill the plan of God for your life. He wants to keep you in that place so that he can continue to wreak havoc in your life and you blame God for it. There is a time and a season for everything (Ecclesiastes 3:1). Now is the season for renewing the mind, determining your path, and moving forward in Christ.

I hear what you're thinking. You're wondering how I can say that understanding the bible is not hard. Well, let me tell you why. What makes it seem hard or difficult to understand is that we try to read it like a history book. We try to understand it in our carnality or natural mind. The carnal (natural) mind can't understand the things of God (spiritual) and that's where we make our mistakes. The carnal mind will never understand spiritual things. We have to read and study from another place. We must first pray and invite the Holy Spirit in.

We have to ask Him to give us the interpretation of the word of God. We have to study the word of God in its context. We have to receive revelation and rhema from the Holy Spirit.

The Holy Spirit will lead us into all truth. We need Him. John 14:26 (AMP) tells us...

> "*But the Helper (Comforter, Advocate, Intercessor—Counselor, Strengthener, Standby), the Holy Spirit, whom the Father will send in My name [in My place, to represent Me and act on My behalf], He will teach you all things. And He will help you remember everything that I have told you.*"

I feel that I need to go here next, when it comes to mindset there is an unhealthy fear based on lies when it comes to the Holy Spirit. In Ephesians 1:13–14 (ESV) it tells us how necessary the Holy Spirit is. *"In him you also, when you heard the word of truth, the gospel of your salvation, and believed in him, were sealed with the promised Holy Spirit, who is the guarantee of our inheritance until we acquire possession of it, to the praise of his glory."*

That is so good, but there is still more, it's called the baptism in the Holy Spirit. (Baptism in the Holy Spirit is different than the indwelling of the Holy Spirit at our conversion and salvation, which was just referenced, that which seals us). We all need the baptism in the Holy Spirit, for this is where we get our power. This is how we obtain the power to live in the world, overcome the world, and do the works that Jesus did and greater works. If Jesus needed the anointing of the Holy Spirit to start his public ministry, (Matthew 3:16), we need Him also. People fear the Holy Spirit because they don't understand Him. They believe that the gift of speaking in tongues is evil, and this is not so. It is our private prayer language and because the devil can't understand it, he does not want us to use it. He can't intercept what we are saying. Praying in tongues is the way that we allow Holy Spirit to intercede on our behalf. When we pray in tongues, we are praying the perfect prayer and praying God's will directly to God. This is an amazing gift.

For anyone who speaks in a tongue does not speak to people but to God. Indeed, no one understands them; they utter mysteries by the Spirit (NIV, 1 Corinthians 14:2). *We also edify ourselves and build ourselves up when we pray in tongues* (1 Corinthians 14:4).

Allow the Holy Spirit to do the inward work that needs to be done in you. Don't be afraid of Him. He is the promise of God. He is a great and awesome gift from God (Luke 11:13). He is the third Person in the Trinity. It is He that empowers us to live holy (Acts 1:8; Romans 8:26; Galatians 5:16), to operate in the fullness of the gifts of the Spirit (Romans 12:6-8; 1 Corinthians 12:8-10), the fullness of the fruit of the Spirit (Galatians 5:22-23) and the wisdom of God (James 1:5). Don't shy away from the baptism of Holy Spirit. We need Him. It is He that reveals to us the mind of Christ. Don't continue to believe the lies of the enemy that tells you that speaking in tongues is evil and that it doesn't take all of that. The devil wants you to believe those lies because he knows that if you receive the truth and you truly step into who you really are and all that God has for you, you will be a real threat to his kingdom. You won't play with him anymore and you won't entertain evil and call it good.

Knowing, understanding, and believing this is critical because, Holy Spirit plays a major part in our identity. We have to get that settled in our hearts. Every good and perfect gift comes from God. God is not evil. He does not do evil things. We have to recognize and welcome the gifts of God so that we can be empowered with what we need to impact the world for God's glory. Believers, it's time to get off the bottle and start growing and maturing. It's time to start digesting some meat (Hebrews 5:12). Get off the fence of offense so that you can start becoming who you were meant to be.

I don't want to deceive anyone into thinking that life is going to be a bed of roses when you step into who God created you to be. When you truly step into who God says you are and start doing what God has called you to do you will notice that you will not be as popular with the world as you once were. Jesus stated it in John 15:18-21 "*If the world hates you, know that it has hated me before it hated you. If you were of the world, the world would love you as its own; but because you are not of the world, but I chose you out of the world, therefore the world hates you. Remember the word that I said to you: 'A servant is not greater than his master.' If they persecuted me, they will also persecute you. If they kept my word, they will also keep yours. But all these things they will do to you on account of my name because they do not know him who sent me.*" He also warns his disciples in John 16 that a time is coming that whoever kills them will believe they are doing God's service and it's because they don't know the Father or Jesus. I don't say this to scare you but I need you to know that choosing to step into who God created you to be is going to cost you something. You may lose friends; you may have to sacrifice some things that you hold very dear to you. You may even lose your life for the cause of Christ.

We learn all of this when we start to study the word of God. Again, knowing the word of God is crucial. "*Be diligent to present yourself approved to God, a worker who does not need to be ashamed, rightly dividing the word of truth*" (NKJV, 2 Timothy 2:15). You will never know your true identity nor be able to grow into who you truly are apart from relationship with God, study of His word and the power of the Holy Spirit. Again, God is in the transforming business and this gospel is all about relationship with Him and the transformation He desires to do in us so that we can become and do all that He has created us to do. Walk by faith and not by sight because without faith it's impossible to please God (Hebrews 11:6). Once you have received the free gift of salvation, deciding to make the identity shift by faith is the next step to crossing over to kingdom. God will do the transforming as you surrender to Him.

Take some time to reflect on this chapter. What are some things that stood out to you that you need to learn more about or shift your mindset on?

9

LIMITING BELIEFS AND HOW TO RECOGNIZE THEM

I believe that identity and mindset are everything and if we don't allow our minds to be renewed through the word of God we will not know, understand or embrace who we are nor be able to walk in who we are in Christ. Back when I was younger, I didn't have the mindset that I have today. I had a defeating mindset. I had a mindset that kept me stuck, that kept me in bondage to things in my past, to the things that I saw which hindered me from walking in faith and yes even as an evangelist. You see I was already licensed and ordained when I contemplated suicide. I was not walking by faith. I was walking by what I saw, what I heard, what I felt, and the fear was gripping and tormenting. I was angry and I was hurt and confused. What I thought I knew about the word of God went right out of the window. I was not yet rooted and grounded. I knew some of it in my head but it had not taken root in my heart yet. My mindset had not yet been renewed and even though some transformation had begun to take place I was stunting my growth. That's right I was stunting my growth. You see, I didn't study as much as I should have. I believed what I heard others teach and preach and thought that was enough. It wasn't enough for me and trust me it's not enough for you either.

I'm not here to tell you that I've arrived because I haven't. I still deal with limiting beliefs, beliefs that seek to constrain me in some way, causing me to not do or say things that I know I should do or say or to do and say things that I shouldn't. The difference today versus my yesterday is that now I can recognize those limiting beliefs and deal with them. As I grow in the word and get stronger in my faith, choosing to do what is right becomes my only option. My integrity outweighs the temptation to give in to the limiting beliefs or to do what I know is wrong. You too are dealing with limiting beliefs; you just don't recognize them as such. You may be triggered by something that will awaken something that is buried deep down inside of you and you have to decide how to deal with it. Learning how to recognize the limiting beliefs and how to deal with them is key. I want to equip you with the tools to do just that, recognize and conquer.

What are limiting beliefs and how do we recognize them?

Limiting beliefs are beliefs that we have that limit us in some way. They are lies that tell us all the reasons why something is not possible for us. They are mental strongholds that surface in the form of destructive, negative behaviors. These limiting beliefs can be about anything in life. Sometimes it's about how you view yourself, other people, or the world in general. It stops you from taking action towards those things that are positive, productive, and that leads to success.

We form our limiting beliefs by observing and learning how things work in our society, through media, by observing others in our environment, through our experiences, and our upbringing. It could surface in the form of something that someone said to us and we believed it or something that happened to us in our relationships and even in a traumatic experience that may have occurred.

How do we recognize them?

They can show up in the form of negative statements. When we are dealing with confrontational people, we may make negative statements. These individuals are doing things that we don't like so we say something negative because their action may have triggered a past hurt, and our protective mechanisms of returning hurt for hurt is the way we learned to deal with it.

Then there are those uncomfortable feelings. Have you ever been getting ready to do something and you have this overwhelming fear, nervousness, or uneasiness about a certain thing or a certain situation? You wondered where that feeling came from, and ask yourself why do I feel this way about that particular thing? Or you can just be sitting, doing nothing and a feeling comes over you and you wonder why you're feeling that way. Then there are those fears, for no apparent reason. It comes from out of nowhere and you wonder why you are fearful about something that you should not be fearful of. It may be surfacing due to something that has happened in your past that is causing you to feel that way. There may be other reasons, but we are talking strictly about limiting beliefs.

What you need to do when these kinds of things happen is start asking questions. Start asking God why you are feeling the way you are feeling. Why is this so uncomfortable? Allow Him to tell you. He will begin to reveal to you what those things are that are embedded deep within your subconscious. Some things you may already be aware of.

I remember having a conversation with a young man about mindset. We talked about our childhood and things that we've seen and heard and experienced in our lives and how it has caused us to develop these limiting beliefs and we carry them throughout our adult life. As I was talking to him, he recognized that he has a limiting belief about relationships because his parents went through divorce. They had a lot of challenges in their relationship and he has challenges in relationships as well. His challenges are based on what he has seen and what he has experienced in his parent's relationship. Because of this, he believes he'll never have a good relationship and that he'll always struggle in that area. We continued to talk about it and by the end of our conversation, he recognized where his limiting beliefs about relationships come from. He said that before I said anything, he didn't recognize it, so now he knows how to deal with it, because now he recognizes that it's something that is holding him back. That was the thing that was causing interruptions in his relationships.

Getting to the root of those limiting beliefs is so critical. This young man was able to get to the root of his struggle in relationships and then begin to work through those limiting beliefs. He realized that just because it happened to his parents it does not have to be his lot in life.

Examples of limiting beliefs come in the form of words like:

"I can't…," Instead of using the words I can't try saying something like, ok, this is not an area that I'm well versed in but what is it that I can do or how can I change that?

"I don't have…," We most often look at the negative. We need to start focusing on the positive instead of the negative. What is it that I do have? What is it that is going to keep me moving forward, keep me progressing instead of something that's going to hold me back?

"This always…," when we use the words "this always," for example "every time I try to do something, this always happens to me." If you continue to use the words this always, guess what? That is going to always keep happening to you. You are speaking that into existence. You're welcoming that into your life. If you want positive things to start happening in your life then you have to focus on the positive and start speaking the positive.

I'm broke…," when you speak "I'm broke" you're speaking poverty into your life. Yes, you may not have the money at the time, but instead of saying I'm broke, just say something like, well, my money is assigned to something else right now, but let me see what I can do. Or, let's see what I can do to come up with what I need in order to be able to do that and then ask God to help you come up with some kind of creative idea. What can you sell or what else can you do (legally, lol) that will help you generate the money you need?

Then there are simple words like "just" and "only". On the surface there appears to be nothing wrong with using these words, but when we use these words, we typically use them to diminish or minimize what we have done. Learn how to enjoy and celebrate your accomplishments no matter how big or small they are. Whatever you have done, you have taken a step forward and that is to be commended.

Limiting beliefs affect every area of our lives, including our physical, mental, spiritual, financial, and emotional health and wellbeing. Limiting beliefs can cause depression, stress, shame, anxiety, panic attacks, grief, phobias, and post-traumatic stress. It can cause all of these things because we focus on the wrong things and then we say the wrong things. Remember *"Death and life are in the power of the tongue, and those who love it will eat its fruit"* (NKJV, Proverbs 18:21).

When you see someone slouching, face always to the ground when they walk, (being aware of customs) they give little to no eye contact, they have unhealthy weight gain/weight loss, or some kind of physical manifestation of a limiting belief, you can see it on them. You can see that they have low self-esteem, or they may have a very poor self-image. Understand that limiting beliefs can bring about the manifestation of some things that you would rather not have in your life. So, if you have some negative manifestations in your life, evaluate where they may be coming from so that you can deal with them and kill them at the root. One example could be emotional eating. Where did it start? When did it start? What kind of problems is the emotional eating causing? What kind of problem do you believe the emotional eating is solving? What steps do you have to take to bring healing in these areas? What action steps are needed to eliminate the emotional eating? There may be someone you need to forgive for hurting you? Go ahead forgive. Who can you call on to support you as you go through the process and keep you accountable?

You can change your life by changing your words and by transforming your mindset with the word of God. Watch the words that you speak. Recognize that words have power and once released into the atmosphere they begin the process of taking shape and manifesting in your life or the life of others. Matthew 15:11 says that *"it's not what goes into the mouth but what comes out of the mouth that defiles a man."*

Our words can become self-fulfilling prophecies (Proverbs 18:21). The negative words you speak are all manifestations of limiting beliefs so be mindful of what you are speaking. Seemingly good things may sound good and politically correct but can be the product of a limiting belief, be careful about just saying things because they sound good. Understand that what you speak and what you believe will change the trajectory of your life, whether good or bad. If you are believing the word of God and speaking His truth, the trajectory of your life will shift. So, make sure that what you are speaking and what you believe line up with the truth of God's word.

10

HOW TO OVERCOME LIMITING BELIEFS

1. Recognize that you have the power to change your mindset.

You have the power to change the direction that your life is going in. That power is called CHOICE. You always have a choice and when you choose to not make a choice, recognize and understand that you have made a choice. That choice may be to stay exactly where you are and not change. Own your power of choice and make it count. Phil 2:5 says, *"Let this mind be in you which is also in Christ Jesus."* This is all about mindset. The word of God tells us that we have the mind of Christ (1 Cor. 2:16). We can know the mind of Christ because if we are a believer in Christ the Holy Spirit lives inside of us. God is a Triune Being. He made us triune beings as well. He is Father, Son, and Holy Spirit. We are spirit, soul, and body. When His Spirit comes to live inside of us His Spirit is closely tied to our spirit and His Spirit reveals. Another scripture that tells us that our mindset is important is Romans 12:2 *"Be not conformed to this world but be transformed by the renewing of your mind so that you may prove what is that good and perfect will of God."* Our minds must be renewed. We can't go on what we have seen, heard, or experienced. God wants us to have a more positive mindset and a better outlook on life and He tells us in His word exactly what we need to focus on in Philippians 4:8 which says, *"whatever is true, whatever is honorable, whatever is just, whatever is pure, whatever is lovely, whatever is commendable, if there is any excellence, if there is anything worthy of praise, think about these things."* He wants us to walk in His wisdom, and in James 1:5, He says that if we lack wisdom, we should ask for it. How awesome is that? God loves us enough to give us the secrets to having a healthy, productive mindset which leads to a healthy productive life. This is how we begin to change our lives. It comes from being in relationship with the Father.

2. Meditation and Prayer.

The goal of Christian meditation is to internalize and personalize the Scripture so that its truth can affect how we think, our attitudes, and how we live, our actions. Christianity is a lifestyle and these disciplines are important in our lives. When we are in relationship with God our lives truly do change. We allow Him to be Lord of our lives and not just Savior. This allows Him to come in and transform us and change our thinking and change the way we respond to the things that go on in our lives, showing us who we truly are in Him. Adding meditation helps you focus on the word so that you can know the truth and not just what you see in front of you which may not be the truth at all. By meditating on the word of God it begins to take root and grow, becoming a part of you. This is so important if we are ever going to live in this world successfully.

Prayer is simply talking to God. It is us communicating with Him and allowing Him to speak to us. Prayer is a dialog, not a monologue. It is two-way communication. We don't have to be afraid to approach God in prayer especially when we miss it. We tend to run away and hide because of the shame and guilt we feel when we mess up. God already knows all about us. Our lives have already been played out before Him. There is nothing that we can do that is a surprise to Him. Shame, guilt, and condemnation are not from God. He has already forgiven us. Jesus paid the full sin debt, all of it, totally and completely. He tells us to come boldly before His throne. He says that if we confess our sins, He is faithful and just to forgive us and to cleans us from all unrighteousness.

Prayer and repentance keep us connected to God. If we neglect these things then we separate ourselves. Do you have a limiting belief that keeps you from approaching God in prayer? Write it down here and seek God about it.

____

____

____

____

____

____

____

Knowing the promises of God helps tremendously in prayer. *"For all the promises of God in Him are Yes, and in Him Amen, to the glory of God through us."* (NKJV, 2 Cor. 1:20) This is why it's important to know the word of God. Do you know His promises to you?

What is one promise in His word that you stand on?

____

____

____

____

____

____

____

____

Next you want to apply scripture. The word of God is what we use to renew our minds so that our lives can be transformed. It tells us this in Romans 12:2, which I shared earlier.

The word of God is living and it's powerful. It will find you and meet you right where you are. This is how powerful it is:

> *"For the word of God is living and active, sharper than any two-edged sword, piercing to the division of soul and of spirit, of joints and of marrow, and discerning the thoughts and intentions of the heart"* (ESV, Hebrews 4:12).

It's important to look up and write down scripture that talks about the thoughts, renewing your mind, your identity, wisdom, and the promises of God because the word of God searches our hearts and will find the lies that we are believing and demolish them because it is able to discern the thought and intentions of our hearts. I talked about the necessity of meditation above. Scripture and meditation go hand in hand. It is also important because in doing so we are feeding ourselves good food and the word will begin to be rooted and grounded within us and it will become so much a part of us as we grow into the person we were created to be. Just like our physical body needs food to survive our spirit also needs food. The word of God is what feeds our spirit. Remember most of us feed our bodies three meals a day. How often do we feed our spirit? Our spirit often goes neglected for long periods of time, starving to death, literally.

It's important to speak the word of God out loud as you're meditating on it. *"So then faith comes by hearing, and hearing by the word of God"* (NKJV, Romans 10:17). As you hear the word your faith increases. As you speak the word this is your faith confession.

Personalizing the scripture makes it more applicable and real to you. There are scriptures that I recite and replace the nouns and pronouns with my name. The promises of God are to His children, so it helps me to know that what I am mediating on and affirming over my life is truly for me.

Try practicing this for yourself.

I ________________ have the mind of Christ because the Holy Spirit lives in me and He reveals it to me. (1 Corinthians 2:16)

Now write down a couple of your own.

____

____

____

____

____

____

____

____

It's important to have an arsenal of scriptures and apply them to your life. There is a constant war going on in the spirit realm. *"For we wrestle not against flesh and blood, but against principalities, against powers, against the rulers of the darkness of this world, against spiritual wickedness in high places"* (KJV, Ephesians 6:12). One of the big lies that the enemy wants us to continue to believe is that we have to fight each other. We get so focused on what people are doing and we want to strike out against them but in reality, there is another force at work and his job is to steal, kill and destroy and He uses people to do that. So, start fighting the real enemy. This is why it's important to know the word of God. His word reveals to us who to fight and how to fight. This is also why it's important to have a relationship with the Father.

God has given us weapons to use to fight effectively and win.

> *"For though we walk in the flesh, we do not war according to the flesh. For the weapons of our warfare are not carnal but mighty in God for*

> *pulling down strongholds, casting down arguments and every high thing that exalts itself against the knowledge of God, bringing every thought into captivity to the obedience of Christ, and being ready to punish all disobedience when your obedience is fulfilled"* (NKJV, 2 Corinthians 10:3-6).

Can you see why the word of God is so important to us walking in our identity and conquering those limiting beliefs? The word of God is our identity. We can't live apart from God nor can we develop into our true selves if we don't have relationship with Him. We will never know who we are, what our purpose is or how to live successfully in this world without relationship with the Father. I keep repeating that because we have to get it. Having the right mindset is a top priority in this journey that we are on.

When you start to recognize those limiting beliefs/lies you need to replace it with the word of God. Always have the word of God that you're standing on so that when things are happening in your life you have your tool kit to fight with. Remember what I shared about my story and how I responded, not being rooted in grounded in His word. Have His word always before your eyes and hidden in your heart so that when things are coming against you and everything looks contrary to what the word of God is saying you can still stand on the word.

Romans 4:19-21 says "*And not being weak in faith, he [Abraham] not considering his own body, already dead (since he was about a hundred years old), and the deadness of Sarah's womb. He did not waver at the promise of God through unbelief, but was strengthened in faith, giving glory to God, and being fully convinced [persuaded] that what He had promised He was also able to perform."* This is faith. Being fully persuaded even though we don't see how somethings can ever be possible we choose to believe God anyway.

3. Affirmations

Remember death and life are in the power of the tongue. It's important that we speak those things that we desire to see come to pass in our lives. Affirming the word of God over our lives, being consistent and standing firm on it.

4. Visualization

You want to see yourself with what it is you are believing God for before you get it. You want to also see yourself doing what it is you are believing for. Seeing yourself walking it out step by step aids in your ability to actually manifest your dreams and goals. This is forming a mental image of something. What is it that you want to see manifest? Make sure that you write things down. Write down what action steps you need to take as you await the manifestation? Do you need to learn another skill? Do you need to improve your skills or go back to school? Do you need to raise money? After you write it down then put it into action. As you are praying and believing God you have to recognize that you have a part to play. You won't get there without taking action. It's not going to just fall in your lap. God's promises are all yes and amen. But even with that every promise of God requires that you do something in order for that promise to be made manifest in your life. Faith without works is dead. Do something. Move forward.

The word of God says where there is no vision, the people perish but he that keeps the law, happy is he (Proverbs 29:18). Habakkuk 2:2 says to write the vision. You need to make sure you write it down. Without vision you won't know where you're going or how to get there.

After you get the vision and write it down you need to start planning. Proverbs 16:9 says: "A man's heart plans his ways, but the Lord directs his steps." As you plan trust God to order your steps and lead you to the manifestation of the vision He has placed in your heart.

Let me end with this. The word of God has everything we need and is written so that we can securely walk in and obtain our victory. I believe that this scripture provides us with exactly what we need to know in order to conquer limiting beliefs. Meditate on it and follow it and I believe your mindset and your life will be transformed.

> *"Finally, my brethren, be strong in the Lord and in the power of His might. Put on the whole armor of God, that you may be able to stand against the wiles of the devil. For we do not wrestle against flesh and blood, but against principalities, against powers, against the rulers of the darkness of this age, against spiritual hosts of wickedness in the heavenly places. Therefore take up the whole armor of God, that you may be able to withstand in the evil day, and having done all, to stand. Stand therefore, having girded your waist with truth, having put on the breastplate of righteousness, and having shod your feet with the preparation of the gospel of peace; above all, taking the shield of faith with which, you will be able to quench all the fiery darts of the wicked one. And take the helmet of salvation, and the sword of the Spirit, which is the word of God; praying always with all prayer and supplication in the Spirit, being watchful to this end with all perseverance and supplication for all the saints— and for me, that utterance may be given to me, that I may open my mouth boldly to make known the mystery of the gospel, for which I am an ambassador in chains; that in it I may speak boldly, as I ought to speak"* (NKJV, Ephesians 6:10-20).

11

THE EFFECTS OF HAVING NO VISION FOR LIFE

For a lot of people in the world, life is just ho-hum. They get up every day with no real vision for life. Some have no plans for anything at all. Some just want to have fun and no responsibilities. Some have no plan for anything beyond going to work to draw a paycheck so that they can pay their bills. They have ceased to dream or live. They have the mindset that where they are and what they have is all there is. Some have a dream. They envision great things for their life but because of a scarcity mindset they are afraid to take the initiative to pursue those dreams. Then, there are the minority, those that have dared to dream and pursue their dreams. Capturing them and daring to become all that they were meant to become. Which one resonates with you?

We've all heard the sayings, "Blue Monday," "It is what it is," "If it's not one thing it's another," "This is just the way it's going to be," "I got up on the wrong side of the bed" and the list goes on. The attitude with which we approach each day will determine the kind of day we will have. It all starts with our mindset. I know I've talked a lot about mindset but if we don't get this part right nothing else will change.

By changing the way you look at things in your mind you have the power to change the trajectory of your life. Is this your life?

No purpose. No vision.

No true identity.

Floundering through life, doing what I was taught, doing what I was told. No ambition, no goals, no passion for life. Just existing day after day; doing what I need to do to get by.

Need to find a job.

Need to get that money.

Got to get all I can get.

Hustle, hustle, hustle.

Having stuff makes me happy. Having a mate makes me happy. I'm bored. I'm lonely. I'm tired. From the outside looking in, people assume I have everything, but I know something is missing. I'm not fulfilled. All the money, all the sex, all the drugs, all the friends, the status, and all of the stuff I have and still I feel empty. There has got to be something more. I put on this fake smile every day and leave my home and pretend that everything is ok, only to come back home to this. I need, I need, I want, I want… truth is I don't know what I need but I know that there has got to be something more.

I believe that many people in the world feel this way. They just go about life feeling empty and unfulfilled, wondering what they are here for? Is there something more to life than just getting up every day to do the same thing over and over again? Unsure of who they are. Well, there is something more. I hope that through this book you are discovering your true identity, that there is hope, that you do have a purpose, and that God desires nothing but good for you. By the end of this book, I hope you are stirred up so much that you are ready to start that personal journey with

Christ Jesus so that you too can experience all that God has planned for you and discover life, what it means to live.

Discovering who you are and what you are meant to become is so exciting. I remember how I felt when I realized that there was more to life than what I had already experienced. There was a God that loved me more than I could ever imagine. He had a plan for my life that He wanted me to know and live. I have a purpose and God wants a relationship with me so that He can share with me the vision that He has for my life and transform me into the person He created me to be. He wants me to know how He feels about me and who I am in Him. He wants the same for you.

I remember thinking I want all that God has for me. How do I get it? What do I have to do? I was already a born-again believer but I still felt somehow, I had to earn His love or do everything right for God to give me what He desired that I have but I was so wrong. My life changed in ways that I never imagined possible and yours will too. Yes, it will take some effort on your part to get what God has for you but trust me it will be worth it. What kind of effort, you ask? You're going to have to spend time in His word so that you will get to know Him and build a personal and intimate relationship with Him, discover who you are, and all about the promises and inheritance He has for you. You're going to have to spend time in prayer, you talking to Him and then listening to and for Him to find out what He's saying and what He wants to say to you. You're going to have to trust Him and be willing to do what He says, (walking by faith) especially those times that you don't understand.

You're going to have some challenges along the way, everyone does. The only difference is that as believers in Christ, we don't have to face those challenges alone. He will be with us. Are you ready? I hope so. You will discover as your relationship with Him grows He will give you hope and vision for a life that you never imagined possible. It's all part of our identity in Him.

12

YOU CAN BE SECURE IN YOUR SALVATION

As believers, some have the mistaken belief that they have to get saved all over again when they fall short and sin. They believe that they can lose their salvation and that God is mad at them and is somehow punishing them for the sin that they have committed. How do I know? I shared earlier how I believed God was mad at me when I was going through a very challenging time in my life and how I was so wrong.

When this mindset is present you hear things like, "God's not through with me yet, the Lord knows my heart, or I'm trying to live right." To me, this indicates that they don't understand that salvation is through grace alone. It has nothing to do with our works. We can't earn our salvation. Jesus already paid the penalty of our sins. Ephesians 2:8-9 *"For by grace you have been saved through faith, and that not of yourselves; it is the gift of God, not of works, lest anyone should boast."* Part of the problem is that many believers in Christ still believe they have a sinful nature so they make excuses. They don't understand that the old sin nature died with the old man. We are now new creations in Christ old things have passed away and all things have become brand new. We still have sin habits that need to be broken and I believe that through the renewing of the mind and yielding to God's will those habits will begin to break. I shared earlier about how I used profanity and when I turned that sin habit over to God, He broke that habit. Remember God is transforming us into his image and likeness.

God is not surprised when we fall short. He is not looking down on us saying "Oh, no she didn't! I can't believe that she just did that!" No, He already knows and despite our shortcomings if we are in Christ, we have the opportunity to confess our sins, repent, accept His forgiveness, and be cleansed. 1 John 1:9 *"If we confess our sins, He is faithful and just to forgive us our sins and to cleanse us from all unrighteousness."* Notice that it says nothing about begging for forgiveness and promising that you'll never do it again. It says that if we confess, He forgives and cleanses. He has already paid the sin penalty. It is finished. We need to get that in our spirits and do what Paul relates in Philippians 3:13-14 *"Brethren, I do not count myself to have [a]apprehended; but one thing I do, forgetting those things which are behind and reaching forward to those things which are ahead, I press toward the goal for the prize of the upward call of God in Christ Jesus."* Jesus is ever making intercession for us. He knows all things. He already knows our life. The word of God tells us that He knows our end from our beginning. Isaiah 46:10 confirms this, *"declaring the end from the beginning and from ancient times things not yet done, saying, 'My counsel shall stand, and I will accomplish all my purpose...."*

You see God is the original reverse engineer. Before He created anything, He planned it out. He saw it all first and then reverse-engineered it. So, everything that is to come has already been done. Everything we will ever do, we've already done.

There is so much richness in the word of God. Holy Spirit will give us revelation when we invite Him into our study time. Something that was revealed to me that I found fascinating about God being the reverse engineer is that Jesus was crucified before the foundation of the world was. 2 Timothy 1:9 states, *"Who hath saved us, and called us with an holy calling, not according to our works, but according to his own purpose and grace, which was given us in Christ Jesus before the world began,"* isn't that eye opening? It was for me.

When God looks at us, He sees us through the blood of Christ. He sees us as His children. He is a loving Father and He wants the best for us. He is not going to disown us just because we mess up. He is longsuffering, *"The Lord is not slack concerning his promise, as some men count slackness; but is longsuffering to us-ward, not willing that any should perish, but that all should come to repentance"* (KJV, 2 Peter 3:9). He is patient with us. If He wanted to destroy us, He would have. He did it before (Remember Noah and the Ark). If He was fed up and totally disappointed in us to the point that he wanted to wipe us out He would not have sent His son to die for us. He loves all that He created. In the book of Genesis, it tells of how we are created in God's image and likeness and He said it was very good. He wants all to come to repentance but the truth is that not all will choose to accept His free gift of salvation. In choosing not to accept God's free gift people are choosing to remain spiritually separated from Him.

We have to realize that we were given free will, which means that we have choices and we can choose to do right or do wrong. We can choose to accept the free gift of salvation and live or not and remain separated from him. We can also choose to not make a choice which is still making a choice. And based on our choices there can be consequences or rewards. We have to be ready to live with the consequences of our choices.

We can't make bad choices and blame God or other people for the consequences that we have to face. Now don't get me wrong, I understand that we face consequences that are the result of other people's choices, things other people may do to us or against us. Those things we don't necessarily have control over. However, what we do have control over is the way that we choose to respond. Understand that whatever happens in our lives, whatever we are faced with, God is well aware of. We need to understand that this is not a license to sin. We have the power within us to not sin through the power of the Holy Spirit who resides inside of us but, most of us, including me, don't always rely on Him to keep us from giving in to temptation as it is declared in the book of Jude 24-25 and 1 Corinthians

10:13.

The Spirit of the Lord lives in every single believer in Christ. Which means every single believer in Christ is free. *"Now the Lord is the Spirit, and where the Spirit of the Lord is, there is liberty. But we all, with unveiled face, beholding as in a mirror the glory of the Lord, are being transformed into the same image from glory to glory, just as from the Lord, the Spirit"* (2 Corinthians 3:17-18). We have liberty. No longer bound by our past. No longer bound by anything because Christ came that we might have life and have it more abundantly.

This is what the Spirit of the Lord does as recited by Jesus as He proclaimed Himself to be the fulfillment of the prophecy. *"The Spirit of the Lord is upon me, because he has anointed me to proclaim good news to the poor. He has sent me to proclaim liberty to the captive and recovering of sight to the blind, to set at liberty those who are oppressed, to proclaim the year of the Lord's favor"* (Luke 4: 18-19).

Not understanding and being assured of our position in Christ makes us unstable because we will constantly be judging ourselves founded on our past. We don't have to force change in our lives. The Spirit will change us. As we study the word, as we yield to Him, as we allow Him access into our lives, He will transform us into that which we were created to be which is the image and likeness of God. It just takes faith. You have to believe even when it appears that nothing may be happening. God gave me this acronym for FAITH, we have to choose to Fully And Intentionally Trust Him! That's it. It's a choice.

Now that we are in Christ, the bible tells us that we have the mind of Christ, which gives us the ability to think kingdom thoughts. We have the ability to do the works that Jesus did and greater works through the power that comes from the Holy Spirit. God also gives us gifts to use to benefit the kingdom. When we take our eyes off of us and stop focusing on the problems in our lives and seek first His kingdom, He provides for us. He gives us wisdom when we ask for it. He teaches us. He guides us. He gives us the ability to produce wealth and shows us how to solve problems. He has given us dominion in the earth realm. He has given us the power and ability to speak to our situations and circumstances, declaring and decreeing, binding and losing and being able to by faith see things change.

If we have the wrong God image and we are unsure of our salvation, then we will never be able to take hold of all that He has for us. We have to walk by faith and not by sight, we have to know the promises of God and how the kingdom of God operates so that we can take hold of the promises and have true manifestation of the promises in our lives. We can't activate or manifest the promises in our lives if we don't know them. As children of God once we know the promises of God all we need to do is receive them.

Some of the reasons that most of us don't receive answers to our prayers is because first, we don't know the will of God and in that all of God's promises are yes and amen. Second, we don't pray in Faith, we beg and plead instead of going to Him in confidences as children and heirs. Third, we cancel it with our words and fourth, we get impatient because it doesn't happen when or how we think it should happen so we give up and when and if it shows up, we don't recognize it.

The word of God says that we have not because we ask not, James 4:2. All it takes is asking *"ask and it shall be given, seek and we shall find, knock and the door shall be opened."* He said that we must believe that we receive when we pray. Meaning whatever we ask for according to the will of God when we pray, we must believe that we already have it before it actually shows up, being fully persuade (knowing without doubting) that what God said, He is able to perform it. God's word will not return to Him void. He makes good on His promises. He is not a man that he should lie. If He said it, it will surely come to pass. That's what the word of God means when it says, God calls those things that be not as though they were, (because they are).

God is a good and faithful Father. He loves us. He wants the best for us that is why He gave us His best. Trust Him. Trust your position in Him.

If you did what Romans 10:9-10 said, *"that if you confess with your mouth the Lord Jesus and believe in your heart that God has raised Him from the dead, you will be saved. For with the heart one believes unto righteousness, and with the mouth confession is made unto salvation."* This says that you are saved. Trust it by faith.

I remember when I was a child, I would go to church with my grandmother and my aunt Shirley. Almost every time the pastor gave the invitation for salvation, I would go to the alter. I didn't understand that I didn't have to get saved all over again because I did something wrong. I would cry because I was scared that I was going to go to Hell. In my adult life even though I had stopped going to the alter during alter call I still didn't feel secure in my salvation. I would beg and plead with God to forgive me and promise not to do what I did again.

Even though I knew in my head that Jesus had paid the whole sin penalty, there was a disconnection with my heart, and all I had to do was trust in His finished work, repent and keep it moving. I've learned that I have to rely on him, surrender whatever that stronghold (sin), habit, issue is to Him and allow Him to do the work in me to break it. He loves me and He is not going to disown me because I'm dealing with issues. He has been and is going to continue to transform me and help me to be victorious over those issues, so that they are not issues for me anymore. He wants to do the same for you if you will allow Him too.

We as children don't have to beg and plead with God. Get to know God. You will be so glad you did. If you belong to Him and His Spirit has come and made His abode in you, then your life is not your own. It belongs to Him. He protects what belongs to Him. Know and understand that you are sealed (Ephesians 1:13), it's your birthright, it's part of your identity in Christ. It took faith to answer the call to salvation. It's going to take faith to live out your life here on earth and accomplish what it is that God has planned for you. Stand on His word and hold on to your faith.

"My sheep hear My voice, and I know them, and they follow Me. And I give them eternal life, and they shall never perish; neither shall anyone snatch them out of My hand. My Father, who has given them to Me, is greater than all; and no one is able to snatch them out of My Father's hand" (John 10:27-29).

13

DO YOU HAVE THE RIGHT GOD IMAGE?

The bible clearly states in Genesis 1 that we are created in the image of God, the true and living God, the Triune God, God the Father, God the Son, and God the Holy Spirit. Have you ever thought about or even stopped to ask yourself what is meant by God's image? How does being made in God's image impact my life? Most of us have never even given it any thought.

We must have a proper understanding of who God is and what it means to be created in His image. If we don't, we will never understand who we are and what it means to be the person that He created us to be. We will not understand our purpose and calling and we will fall very short of being able to access all that God has prepared and planned for us. We will surely live out our lives in defeat, frustration, anger, and bitterness because there is no life apart from Him.

The condition of the church today makes it quite clear that very few are asking the question, or even understands what it means to be made in God's image? Take a moment to ponder the question. Were you able to confidently say that you have a healthy image of who God is? Having accurate knowledge of who God is, is important if we are to ever know and understand our true identity in Christ.

I believe God impressed upon my heart to write this chapter because there are so many Christians who don't know Him. We have this false perception of who He is. Society and the Church (body of Christ) has given us the perception that God kills babies, inflicts people with illnesses, and causes bad things to happen to good people. They believe that He allows all of these to teach us something, or He is punishing us for something we did wrong. If this is your view of God then you are believing the lies of the enemy, Satan. He wants us to believe those lies because if we do then he comes off as the good guy and he can get us outside of our realm of protection in Christ where he can continue to wreak havoc in our lives and accomplish his mission, which is to steal, to kill and to destroy us. If we believe that God is not good, then we turn our backs on Him and stop listening. Please, please, please understand this, *"The thief comes only to steal and to kill and to destroy. That is Satan. [but take a look at what comes next, Christ says,] I came that they may have life and have it abundantly."* John 10:10

What we fail to understand is that if these are the lies that we are believing then we are not walking in faith but doubt and unbelief and we don't know the God we confess to believe in. We don't believe that God is good. We don't believe that God answers prayer. We don't believe that God will answer our prayers, to be more precise. We pray to hope and not believe. We hope God will do it, but we don't believe He will.

God wants us to know Him because in knowing Him we get a clearer understanding of who we are, why we are here and we get a clearer understanding of what life is and how to live and be in the world and not of the world.

This is how to know if you know God and are in Him: 1 John 4:8 says, *"He who does not love does not know God, for God is love."* and 1 Corinthians 13:13, says, *"And now abide faith, hope, love, these three; but the greatest of these is love."* God is love. So, when we walk in love, we are portraying the image of God.

Love is an important part of our identity. Without it, we cease to be salt and light in a dark and dying world. The sad reality is that religion and the stigma that it has created has put a dark cloud over what being in Christ means. The world looks at Christianity or being a believer in Christ as being hypocritical, judgmental, and in some cases hateful. They don't understand that there is a difference between being religious and being in Christ. Christianity is all about the relationship with God through Christ. Religion is about laws and rules and a belief in or worship of something or someone greater than themselves, not necessarily God. If we look throughout the New Testament scriptures it was the religious leaders that Jesus seemed to have an issue with. It was the religious leaders that sought to find fault with everything He did. In my opinion, the practice of religion and not relationships seek to find fault in everything that people do. It's not about love, grace, forgiveness, reconciliation, restoration, or mercy it's about judgment and condemnation. When we truly know Him, we imitate Him in the world by living out His characteristics in the world and showing love, grace, forgiveness, reconciliation, restoration, and mercy.

Matthew 5:13-16 tells us what we should look like to the world...

> *"You are the salt of the earth, but if salt has lost its taste, how shall its saltiness be restored? It is no longer good for anything except to be thrown out and trampled under people's feet.*
>
> *You are the light of the world. A city set on a hill cannot be hidden. Nor do people light a lamp and put it under a basket, but on a stand, and it gives light to all in the house. In the same way, let your light shine before others, so that they may see your good works and give glory to your Father who is in heaven."*

We should be doing good works in the world, being salt and light.

Everything we do should bring God glory. When we live like this it represents the image of God. It shows that we know Him.

Now that you see how important this subject is, let's take a few moments to talk about God's image. God is love but He is also a just judge and a God of justice. He is a faithful and loving Father. God is omniscient(all-knowing), omnipotent (all-powerful, almighty), and omnipresent (present everywhere). He has no beginning and He has no end. Revelations 1:8 states, *"I am the Alpha and the Omega, says the Lord God, who is and who was, and who is to come. The Almighty."* We have to begin to see Him that way to receive from Him. We have to truly know Him for ourselves. We can't just know about Him. We have to know Him intimately. We have to develop a personal and intimate relationship with Him. We have to study His word so that we know His character and we develop the skill of recognizing His voice.

What is character?

It is "moral excellence and firmness" according to Merriam-Webster.

What is God's character?

God's character is found throughout His word. I believe the fruit of the Spirit is one of the ways God's character is described. They are found in Galatians 5:22-23, *"But the fruit of the Spirit is love, joy, peace, longsuffering, kindness, goodness, faithfulness, gentleness, self-control...,"* these are characteristics that are important for us to nurture and grow in. As we do, we look more and more like Him. I believe God will help us to develop and grow this fruit as He continues the good work, He has begun in us.

When God gives us a commandment or a statute to follow, He is not trying to keep us from enjoying life. It is just the opposite. He is teaching us what it means to have life and to have it in abundance, He is teaching us what it means to be made in His image and likeness, and how to exhibit His character and be representative of the kingdom, our royal heritage. I believe that He is protecting us from dangers that we are not aware of. Next time you sit down to have communion with God and study His word, go into it with an understanding that God wants to not only work something great in you, He also wants to get something great to you.

It is through the study of God's word and spending time in His presence that we get to know Him, understand who we are and how to walk it out in the world. I believe if you make it a priority to develop these disciplines you will grow in your knowledge of Him and also understand yourself better in the process.

14
INTIMATE MOMENTS

Any relationship worth having needs to be nurtured. This requires time alone with that special someone so that you can interact, talk and get to know each other. Remember when you met that special someone and all you wanted to do was to spend time with him or her? You thought about that person constantly. You fell head over hills quickly. You couldn't get enough of spending time in that person's presence. The more time you spent together, the more you learned about them and the more they learned about you. But that is not the only thing that was happening as you were spending quality time together. Something else just as significant was taking place. It's something that we tend to overlook in our relationships with other people. What I'm referring to is the fact that we also learn a lot about ourselves in the process. The subject of intimacy plays a vital role in learning about our identity. Without intimacy, there is no way we will ever discover who we truly are and what our purpose in life is.

There are several accounts in the bible about how important intimacy is in the process of becoming who we are meant to be and fulfilling purpose in our lives. The most important one is Jesus' relationship with the Father. Jesus came to earth for a very specific purpose. This is also true for us. Jesus knew his purpose and He knew that intimacy with the Father was very necessary to fulfill His purpose. He knew exactly who He was and He walked in it daily. Jesus spent intimate moments with the Father to get direction for His life. He was focused and disciplined. This is what it is going to take in order for us to discover who we are and be confident in our identity so that we can fulfill purpose in our lives. I know, I know, you don't like the "D" word, "Discipline. This is a word that Jesus has been placing on my heart lately.

Merriam Webster defines it this way, "orderly or prescribed conduct or pattern of behavior."

Some of the most successful people in the world became successful because they disciplined themselves. We need to develop discipline in our lives so that we can accomplish the things that we need to accomplish in the world. The most important discipline is regular consistent time spent with the Father.

Jesus was disciplined. He got up early in the morning and spent time with the Father. He worshiped the Father and got instruction for the day. He gave God the first fruits of His day. We read account after account of Jesus getting away to spend time with the Father. Jesus and the Father were so intimate that He and the Father were one and Jesus could do nothing of himself. Jesus said...

> *"I speak to you timeless truth. The Son is not able to do anything from himself or through my initiative. I only do the works that I see the Father doing, for the Son does the same works as his Father. Because the Father loves his Son so much, he always reveals to me everything that he is about to do. And you will all be amazed when he shows me even greater works than what you've seen so far!"* (TPT, John 5:19-20).

Jesus relied on God the Father for instruction and direction as He continued on His journey.

There are others mentioned in the bible who had amazing relationships with the Father. Abraham, Isaac, Jacob, David, Noah, and Moses are notable ones.

It's in those intimate moments with the Father that He begins to reveal His truth to us. It is in those moments where we get to know God and He reveals our true identity to us. He enlightens us about who we are and what He desires for us. Each of the people I mentioned above had a special relationship with God. God talked with them. They talked with God. They got their assignments and instructions from God as they fulfilled purpose in their lives. They were able to have victory in their lives because they did not depend on or rely on themselves. They trusted God and God always came through on their behalf. God wants to do the same thing for us. He wants us to know who we are in Him because in doing so we can live in victory knowing that God is always working behind the scenes even when it doesn't look like it.

Joseph is a good example to use here. Joseph was his father's favorite. His brothers despised him because of it. God gave Joseph a dream. He shared it with his family. This did not help the situation. His brothers ended up selling him into slavery. Joseph then ended up being accused of rape by Potiphar's wife and was thrown into prison. By all accounts, Joseph could have complained and blamed God for all that was happening in his life. He could have said this is not fair, why is all of this happening to me. I didn't do anything wrong, but he didn't. He kept a great attitude throughout all that he had endured. He surely could not see how the dream that God gave him was ever going to come to pass. He had no idea what God was working in the background.

Everything that was happening to him was meant for his bad but God worked it all for his good. God knew that his brothers were going to sell him into slavery. God knew that Potiphar's wife was going to accuse him. God knew who Joseph would meet in prison and he used all of that to bring the dream and his plan for Joseph to pass and Joseph fulfilled the purpose for which he was sent.

When we develop intimacy with God and keep our eyes on Him, allow

Him to do the work that needs to be done in us, follow His directions, and keep his commands we will grow into the image and likeness that we were created to be (2 Corinthians 3:18). It is our relationship with Him and those intimate moments that we spend in prayer, praise, worship and time in the word that enables us to stand in the face of all that we may encounter and endure and come out victorious.

God, the Creator of all things had you in mind before the beginning of time. If you are a living, breathing human being you are not here by mistake. God knew you before you were formed in your mother's womb. He created you with purpose in mind and He put in you an innate desire for something greater than yourself and that desire is for a relationship with Him. It is only through our relationship with Him that we come to realize the truth about who He is, who we are in Him, and why we exist in this world.

If you have accepted Jesus as Lord and Savior of your life and you are comfortable with just being saved and knowing that you are going to heaven someday, but you've never developed a relationship with God then I encourage you to make that a priority in your life.

Salvation is just the beginning of your faith journey. If you get there and that is where you stay you will be missing out on all of the other glorious benefits of being an heir in God's kingdom. There is so much more to this kingdom journey than just being saved and going to heaven someday. Christianity is all about our relationship with the Father through Jesus Christ making our relationship with God personal and intimate.

Knowing how much God loves you and how much He wants to commune with you is the start of a beautiful relationship, that special Father-child relationship. Even if you don't have a good relationship with your natural parents, or if you've never met your natural parents, you need to know that God wants to fill that void and show you what real unconditional love is all about.

He desires to spend quality intimate time with you. When we allow

Him to do the work in our lives that He has planned He will transform us and lead us into a life that is beyond anything we could have ever imagined. He desires that we prosper and be in health. He desires that we live a life of abundance and we experience all that the kingdom of God has to offer. That only comes through a relationship with Him.

Take a few moments and think about your relationship with Him. Do you have one? Is it as intimate as you desire it to be? What can you do to improve it?

15
HONOR THE HOUSE

How many of you own a home? My husband and I do and we strive to take good care of it. Most of us take pride in our homes and take good care of them. We require that when people visit our homes that they respect our homes and not do anything to destroy them. Well just as we take pride in and respect our homes and require others to do the same, the Holy Spirit who's home we are, feels the same way about His house. At times I believe that we often forget that our bodies belong to God and that the Holy Spirit lives within us. In 1 Corinthians 3:16-17, ESV it states, *"Do you not know that you are God's temple and that God's Spirit dwells in you? If anyone destroys God's temple, God will destroy him. For God's temple is holy, and you are that temple."* Likewise, He states in 1 Corinthians 6:19-20, ESV, *"Or do you not know that your body is a temple of the Holy Spirit within you, whom you have from God? You are not your own, for you were bought with a price. So glorify God in your body."*

Our identity includes being the house of God. He considers us holy. *"Be ye holy, for I am holy"* (1 Peter 1:16). It is God who empowers us to be holy and to live holy. Apart from Him, there is no way we can do that. He is the power that does the miraculous work on the inside of us that enables us to live holy. Just as there was nothing we could do to save ourselves we are limited to the changes we can make within ourselves and in our lives.

The work is done from the inside out. If we want real lasting change it has to be done through Christ. He has given us everything pertaining to life and godliness.

At the time of our conversion, He comes in and makes His home in us. How special is that? God thinks so much of us that He would want to make us His home. We want to make sure that we honor the house and make it fit for a King. After all, He moved in so that tells me that He created us to be fit for a King.

There are many things that we do that don't honor God's house but I want to start with the one that I believe is most popular and I'm sure most everyone can relate to it in some way. Yes, you guessed it. I believe the most popular way that we dishonor our bodies is by having sex outside of marriage. We don't think about the consequences, we want to satisfy our flesh or be liked by that special someone. Very few parents take the time to sit down with their children and explain the importance of waiting until marriage to have sexual relations. There are many reasons, and it would probably take a lifetime to list them all.

Understand this, when God gives the command "do not" in his word, He is not trying to keep us from having fun or trying to keep anything good from us. He wants to protect us. He created sex and it is good but He created it for marriage. When I say marriage, I'm referring to marriage between one woman and one man. Having sex outside of marriage has so many negative consequences and I believe God wants to protect us from those negative consequences. God is all-knowing and He knows what is down the road for us due to the choices that we will make in life. 1 Corinthians 6:18 says, "Flee sexual immorality. Every sin that a man does is outside the body, but he who commits sexual immorality sins against his own body." Not only are we sinning against our bodies, but when a man and a woman enter a sexual relationship for the first time, a blood covenant is formed and we become one flesh with that person (Genesis 2:24, 1 Corinthians 6:16). Women have a hymen. The hymen covers the opening of the vagina. It is usually broken by some sort of penetration and releases blood. Though this may not always happen it is what typically happens. This is I believe, why God intended sex for marriage. He doesn't want us caught up in sin but He also doesn't want us attached in covenant to someone that we may not marry. Sexually transmitted diseases, pregnancy, soul ties, and familiar spirits are consequences of having sexual relations. If we obey God's commands, we save ourselves a lot of unnecessary heartache and pain. I wish someone would have taken the time to explain this to me. Would it have made a difference? Maybe, but at least I would have been armed with more information besides, "keep your legs closed and don't be out there having sex… because I said so."

There are other ways that we dishonor the house of God and bring upon ourselves negative consequences. These include gluttony, abuse of alcohol and drugs, having sexual encounters with someone of the same sex, and doing other unhealthy things to our bodies. Some of us do these things because we have not been educated or made aware of the seriousness of our actions not only in the natural but the spiritual ramifications as well. Some of us do these things because of fear, insecurity, or unhealthy emotional attachments and some do it out of rebellion.

If we desire to honor the house of God, it is through the power of God within us that we will be able to do that. The same power that raised Jesus from the dead is the same power that resides in us, that Holy Spirit power that can keep us from falling and present us blameless before God. Wow, did you get that? Holy Spirit will keep us if you ask Him too, if we yield to Him and allow Him to. That is the way we honor the house of God, by allowing Him to work in us through the power of the Holy Spirit. What an amazing God we serve. He gives us the power to do what it is that He desires us to do. He gave us the power to do that which we could never do on our own. Thank God, we don't have to do it on our own or in our strength. He wants us to be victorious so He empowers us to do just that.

When I came to myself (after going through what I call my crazy season, that season where I was struggling with my identity and giving myself away due to all of my insecurities and fears), and I learned to surrender all of the hurt, pain, anger, disappointment, confusion, emotions, everything to God, that is when things started to change. I stopped trying to do it all on my own. I started purposely spending time in God's presence, listening as I studied His word. Learning to hear Him and allow Him to do what He needed to do in me as He taught me how to love myself, respect myself and honor His house. It didn't happen overnight. It took time. My flesh and my spirit were at constant war. It's still at war but in a different way. My flesh never wants to surrender but I'm learning to take control and put my flesh under submission. We have to learn how to tell our flesh no (1 Thessalonians 4:3-5).

We all have routine things we do in life that take no thought when doing them. They become automatic. One particular morning I did just that. I got up and got ready for work. I put my Bluetooth in my ear and turned it on as I normally do. I heard the words "power on, connected." Something happened at that moment that caught me totally off guard. I heard this still small voice (which I believe to be God) on the inside of me repeat, "power on, connected." But what came after that surprised me. The voice continued "what are you connected to? The power is always on but are you connected?" I began to press into that and think about it intently. How often do I get up and do things in my strength and power and not even acknowledge the power that resides on the inside of me? Yes, the power is always on, but do I always connect? My answer was no. The voice reminded me that the Holy Spirit is alive in me and that He is there to help me. He is my Helper, my Guide, my Strength, He leads me, He directs my path, He instructs me in the everyday things of life when I'm not sure what to do. He reveals things to me that I would not otherwise know. The point I am making here is this. Power is needed if we are going to be successful in making an impact in the world. Power is needed if we are going to be successful at changing our lives. Just like a lamp needs to be plugged into a power source to shine or a computer needs to be charged to work properly, we as believers in Christ need to charge our spiritual batteries by staying connected or plugged into our power source so that we can make changes in our lives and in the world for the glory of God. This is the only way we can make an impact in the world that is lasting and life-changing for the kingdom of God. Honoring the house of God (our bodies) is one of the ways we do that. We allow ourselves to stay fully connected when we remain free from sin, take care of our bodies, we only get one, honor it, protect it, respect it, and require others to do the same. Remember, if you are in Christ your body is no longer yours but God's. That is our identity.

16

GOD'S WAYS ARE NOT OUR WAYS

> *"For My thoughts are not your thoughts, Nor are your ways My ways," says the Lord.*
>
> *"For as the heavens are higher than the earth, So are My ways higher than your ways, And My thoughts than your thoughts"* (NKJV, Isaiah 55:8-9).

This is a tough subject and honestly, I didn't want to address it but God would not allow me to leave it out. God would not let me rest so I tried to address it by just mentioning it within the previous chapter. God continued to impress upon me that He wants a chapter dedicated to this particular subject and I believe it's because He loves us so much that He does not want us confused about who we are nor does he want us to be destroyed for lack of knowledge (Hosea 4:6). So, I approach this subject in the spirit of love that God who is Love intended.

Let me be very clear here, GOD LOVES PEOPLE! When He looked around at everything He had made He said that what He had made was very good. That included us. He gave us His best and He desires that we live in obedience to His commands so that we can receive all of the good things He has prepared for us. Obedience to the word of God is a requirement. It's not optional.

In Chapter 15, the chapter on Honoring the House, I spoke about sexual immorality and my struggle with sexual sin. In this chapter, I want to address another form of sexual sin that grieves God's heart and that is the subject of same-sex relationships (LGBTQ) among those that confess to be believers in Christ or Christians if you will. God was very specific about how He feels about sin, all sin, not just this subject, but sins of the flesh which are addressed in Galatians 5:19-21 and Colossians 3:5, I believe these are important to Him because this too is a sin against our own bodies. I understand that this is where I may lose a lot of you but I have to be obedient to what God is directing me to do. If this is a sore subject area for you, I encourage you to seek God for His truth to you personally. As I stated at the beginning of this book, don't take my word as gospel. Please seek God and study it for yourself. It's okay to ask God directly if you are living your life the way he desires, if it aligns with what His word says or if there are any sin habits in your life that He wants to deal with. You can even come right out and ask Him if he approves of your same-sex sexual relationship. It's okay, He welcomes our questions because He wants us to know His truth.

As ambassadors of God and His kingdom, being made in His image and likeness, we have a responsibility to live our lives in light of God's truth. In other words, the life we live in the flesh reveals God's truth or it destroys our witness and causes people to go astray. The subject of same-sex sexual relationships within the body of Christ is a subject that the body of Christ is not willing to address out of fear of being accused of spreading hate, judgment, and condemnation. We as a body of believers must begin to stand up and speak boldly what God says. It has nothing to do with hate, judgment, or condemnation. It's about LOVE! We have to LOVINGLY tell people the truth. If we remain silent then we do an injustice to the world and the body of Christ. Loving someone is being able to tell them and show them that I can love you and not agree with everything you do or say. I love you enough to tell you the truth. I have friends and family members that are living an LGBTQ lifestyle.

It doesn't make me love them any less just because I don't agree with their lifestyle. I have friends and family members who have chosen to live their lives in other ways that I don't agree with which is outside of the will of God for their lives, but again, it does not make me love them any less. Understand this God loves us unconditionally and we are to love others unconditionally. But just because God loves us unconditionally does not mean that He does not require us to walk in obedience to His word (John 14:15).

The way of the world has blinded us to the ways of God. God created us male and female (Genesis 1:27). He gave Eve to Adam to be his wife. That is God's order for marriage. That is God's order for any relationship that could potentially become a marriage relationship. God created sex. Sex is a gift given for marriage. Sex is good when it is entered into the way that God created it for and that is in the context of a marital relationship between one man and one woman (Genesis 2:24; Hebrews 13:4). God's word is clear. We can't change it. No earthly laws will ever outweigh God's law. Let's face it, not all earthly laws are just and not all earthly laws align with the laws of God. Some earthy laws were made to satisfy the flesh, to fulfill the personal agendas of the ones making the laws, and to be politically correct according to the world's way of thinking and believing.

A house divided against itself cannot stand (Matthew 12:25). God cannot do anything contrary to who He is. Some say that God made them LGBTQ. We are made in His image and likeness. If God speaks against it in His word, He would be divided against Himself to create something contrary to His word. When we live outside of the will of God for our lives we have to live with the consequences of those choices. It is clearly outlined here in Romans 1:18-32...

> *"For the wrath of God is revealed from heaven against all ungodliness and unrighteousness of men, who suppress the truth in unrighteousness, because what may be known of God is manifest in them, for God*

has shown it to them. For since the creation of the world His invisible attributes are clearly seen, being understood by the things that are made, even His eternal power and Godhead, so that they are without excuse, because, although they knew God, they did not glorify Him as God, nor were thankful, but became futile in their thoughts, and their foolish hearts were darkened. Professing to be wise, they became fools, and changed the glory of the incorruptible God into an image made like corruptible man—and birds and four-footed animals and creeping things.

Therefore God also gave them up to uncleanness, in the lusts of their hearts, to dishonor their bodies among themselves, who exchanged the truth of God for the lie, and worshiped and served the creature rather than the Creator, who is blessed forever. Amen.

For this reason God gave them up to vile passions. For even their women exchanged the natural use for what is against nature. Likewise also the men, leaving the natural use of the woman, burned in their lust for one another, men with men committing what is shameful, and receiving in themselves the penalty of their error which was due.

And even as they did not like to retain God in their knowledge, God gave them over to a debased mind, to do those things which are not fitting; being filled with all unrighteousness, sexual immorality, wickedness, covetousness, maliciousness; full of envy, murder, strife, deceit, evil-mindedness; they are whisperers, backbiters, haters of God, violent, proud, boasters, inventors of evil things, disobedient to parents, undiscerning, untrustworthy, unloving, unforgiving, unmerciful; who, knowing the righteous judgment of God, that those who practice such things are deserving of death, not only do the same but also approve of those who practice them."

This is true for any sin not just sexual immorality. God is righteous and just. He is holy and He requires that of us as His children. We have to start being led by the Spirit of God and not our flesh and emotions. That is why out of obedience to God I am adding this chapter. God desires that we know who we are in Him and that we walk in it. He desires that we know the truth because it is His truth that makes us free (John 8:31). Not believing the lie that says we can do whatever we want or live however we want and still be in right standing with God. Sin separates us from God. Sin in our lives, no matter what it is, keeps us from receiving all that God has for us. When we live in disobedience, it's difficult to hear God. When we live in disobedience, we hinder the blessings of God for our lives. As I stated at the beginning of this book and the beginning of this chapter, don't take what I say as gospel. Please research and study for yourself. God reveals His truth to us. We must learn to hear Him. We must learn who He says that we are. We have to be open to hearing from Him and allowing Him to transform us into who He created us to be and not who we believe that we are supposed to be or who the world has dictated to us that we are supposed to be. The choices that we make in life are between us and God. He is the one that we ultimately have to answer to. God loves us. Try Him, I mean really try Him. You will be amazed at what He reveals to you. You will be amazed at His love for you. His Holy Spirit will lovingly convict you, not condemn you. He will lovingly reveal to you, His truth. Understand this, those that practice hate and violence against any people group and say that they are doing it in the name of God are lying and they don't represent the true and living God.

17

THE TRANSITION

When we give our lives to Christ and accept Him as Lord and Savior of our lives, we bring our old habits and mindsets with us. At that moment, however, a transition takes place, we go from being a citizen of this world (earth) to a citizen of the kingdom of God as stated in Eph. 2:19. What is the kingdom of God? It is the place where God rules and reigns. It's a spiritual realm where God has seated us as stated in Eph. 2: 4-7 (ESV) *"But God, being rich in mercy, because of the great love with which he loved us, even when we were dead in our trespasses, made us alive together with Christ—by grace you have been saved— and raised us up with him and seated us with him in the heavenly places in Christ Jesus, so that in the coming ages he might show the immeasurable riches of his grace in kindness toward us in Christ Jesus."* In Luke 17:20-21 (AMP) Jesus explains to the Pharisees that *"The kingdom of God is not coming with signs to be observed or with a visible display; nor will people say, 'Look! Here it is!' or, 'There it is!' For the kingdom of God is among you [because of My presence]."* Because He is present with us and in us, we carry the kingdom of God wherever we go. We have access to whatever we need in the kingdom as we partner with Him to accomplish His will here on earth. We pray *"Your kingdom come. Your will be done on earth as it is in heaven"* (NKJV, Matt. 6:10). In Rom. 14:17 the kingdom of God is described as "righteousness, and peace and joy in the Holy Spirit". In essence we are praying let Your righteousness, and peace and joy in the Holy Spirit come. Your will be done on earth as it is in heaven.

Another transition takes place when we give our lives to Christ. We go from who we were before accepting Christ to the new creation we become in Christ. We no longer have a sinful nature because we take on the nature of Christ and he clothes us in His righteousness.

As we grow in Christ, we begin to unlearn wrong teachings and we learn new habits and develop a new mindset that is grounded in the truth of God's word.

We don't look any different, we may not feel any different but by faith, we have to believe that we are different, that something has changed. We have to believe that we have become a new creation in Christ. The word of God says that "old things are passed away, behold all things have become new." Now begins the journey of learning who we have become, who God is, who we are in Him, and who He is in us. For the transition to become transparent in our lives it requires us to allow Jesus to not only be Savior but to be Lord in our lives. We have to be willing to relinquish our control as we enter this journey of developing a brand-new relationship with God intimately as our loving Father.

Our mindset is the first thing that needs to be dealt with. In Romans, it says that we are *"not to be conformed to this world but transformed by the renewing of our minds so that we may prove what is that good and acceptable will of God."* So, this is a very important step. The way that we do that is by feeding ourselves the word of God regularly. We have to *"study to show ourselves approved a workman that need not be ashamed rightly dividing the word of truth"* (2 Timothy 2:15). The word of God is food for us. It is described as milk (1Peter 2:2) and meat in the bible (Hebrews 5:11-14). Jesus who is the Word, referred to Himself as the bread of life (John 6:35) in scripture.

We can't grow in spirit, in truth, or in strength without the word of

God.

We are spirit beings and our spirits need to eat as well as our physical bodies. We feed our bodies three meals a day but we so very often neglect and starve our spirits.

Another thing that's important to know and understand here as we are transitioning is that we can't just accept everything that is being preached and taught. We are responsible to try the spirit by the Spirit according to 1 John 4:1-5...

> *"Beloved, do not believe every spirit, but test the spirits, whether they are of God; because many false prophets have gone out into the world. By this, you know the Spirit of God: Every spirit that confesses that Jesus Christ has come in the flesh is of God, and every spirit that does not confess that Jesus Christ has come in the flesh is not of God. And this is the spirit of the Antichrist, which you have heard was coming and is now already in the world. You are of God, little children, and have overcome them because He who is in you is greater than he who is in the world. They are of the world. Therefore, they speak as of the world, and the world hears them."*

We have to study the word of God for ourselves. I learned so much wrong doctrine because I was listening to what people were saying or watching how people were living and not checking it out for myself. You see I believed the lies too. The lies that I can't understand the bible. It's too hard to understand. I can't hear God. He doesn't talk to me. All lies!

The bible is not difficult to understand. The problem is that most people are reading it like a history book and trying to understand it with the carnal, natural mind. You will never understand it that way. You have to invite the Holy Spirit to give you understanding of the Word of God. He is our Helper, our Guide, He reveals and gives us the interpretation of the word of God, the rhema and revelation we need in order to bring about transformation in our lives and the lives of others. You also need the right study tools. God does speak and we can hear Him. The word of God says that out of heaven He has made us to hear his voice (Deuteronomy 4:36). As you train your hearing through study of His word you will begin to recognize Him more and more.

Another thing you have to be careful of is making the mistake of studying the word based on what you were taught and missing the revelation that the Holy Spirit wants to give you. I did that a lot until I learned to ask the Holy Spirit questions and recognize God's voice as I was studying. Not that I am always 100% sure of what I'm hearing? No, nobody is, but time spent with Him helps us to more easily recognize Him than if we had not been spending time with Him at all. If it is Him it will prove to be true as it becomes a reality. If it doesn't, keep trusting that He will make it clear to you. I want you to also be aware that you have to go into your study time with an open mind, a receptive heart and an expectation to receive so that you can hear from the Holy Spirit. Another thing that helps is using other study tools. I had to learn how to use other study tools, like a concordance, bible dictionary, commentaries, etc. Yes, it's going to take some effort on your part but it is so worth it.

I was a minister of the gospel when I went through my identity crisis. I've said it before, I thought I knew God, but I discovered that I didn't know Him as I thought. Sure, I knew his voice to some degree. I had heard Him several times before so I was able to recognize His voice when He stopped me from swallowing a handful of pills as I contemplated suicide. But I didn't know Him as intimately as I desired to know Him. I could quote a few scriptures and thought I believed them until I started going through one of the most difficult times in my life. I lost it. I said this earlier, but I'm going to repeat it. I always thought God was angry with me because I kept messing up. I would repent and apologize and say I wasn't going to do it again only to repeat those same old bad habits over and over again. I didn't understand that the same reason I needed God in the first place was the reason I need Him throughout this journey. In my flesh I am incapable of living a sinless life. In my flesh I was incapable of bringing lasting change to my life or becoming who He created me to be. It is only through the power within me (Holy Spirit) that I can break those habits and become who I am created to be. Jesus already took care of the sin issue. I am no longer a slave to sin. Sin has no power over me. It has no power over you either. Jesus paid it all. Sure, I will still make mistakes and so will you. We all will, but sin cannot destroy us. Jesus says in His word that if we confess our sin, He is faithful and just to forgive us and to cleans us from all unrighteousness. We confess and He forgives and cleanses us. I believe that when we confess and give that habit over to Jesus eventually that habit will no longer have a stronghold in our lives. I know this to be true because I've experienced it.

We have to know who we are and we have to be secure in who we are.

I talk about self- confidence, but when I talk about self-confidence it's not about me having confidence in myself and my own abilities apart from Him. When I say self-confidence, I'm talking about the God-confidence that I have so that I can have confidence in myself. It's the confidence that I have in God, that He has put in me certain gifts, talents and abilities to be able to do what it is He has called and appointed for me to do. So, I can confidently go and do what He says because I have confidence in Him working through me to be able to produce what it is He wants me to produce. My self-confidence is not about me being self-made and my own abilities apart from Him, it's my abilities in Him.

We must have faith. Faith is very necessary if we are ever going to confidently go through life and become all that God has created us to be and do all that God has planned and ordained for us to do. His word says that it is impossible to please Him without faith and faith not attached to works is dead. We all have faith in something. Most often it is misplaced faith. Faith in what we see, what we are currently going through, who others perceive us to be or who we perceive ourselves to be based on what we've experienced or have been told. True faith is in God and His ability to transform us and our situation, faith in the word of God and the God of the word.

You have a choice, you can choose to go on living life as you have been doing up until this point, being so depressed and wanting to give up on life, having no hope or identity apart from people and things outside of you, or you can choose life in Christ and start living the life that God so much desires that you live. Recognizing that you are in the world but you are no longer of the world. You are now resident of another kingdom. The kingdom of God. This is another reason why studying the word of God is important. We as believers in Christ have to start learning what the kingdom of God is and how the kingdom of God operates. Studying the word of God is where it begins. Learn to do things God's way. Remember, God will do the work on the inside of you that needs to be done as He transforms you into who He created you to be. He has begun a good work in you already and the word of God says in Philippians 1:6 "being confident of this very thing, that He who has begun a good work in you will complete it until the day of Jesus Christ;" He is not done with you yet. You have not become the you that He has created you to be so stop focusing on who you are right now as you perceive yourself to be. Who you are is yet to be revealed. The you that He created you to be will blow your mind. This is why we need to stop looking at people thinking we know who they are. We have no idea because, what we see before us is what the world has fooled us into believing that we are. Once God gets our attention and we turn it all over to Him. He is able to finish what He started in us. Trust Him and be amazed as you finally meet the you that you are yet to become. I can say today that I am not the person I was just a few years ago. I have grown and changed and I am standing in awe of how God is transforming me.

I challenge you to start going through the scriptures and writing down scripture that reveal to you your true identity in Christ. Start declaring them out loud every day. You will eventually really start believing as the word of

God becomes more real to you. Let me help you get started.

Eph. 1: 3 I am blessed

Eph 1: 4 I am chosen, holy and blameless before Him

Eph. 1:5 I am a son/daughter

Eph 1:7 I am redeemed and forgiven

Eph. 1: 13 I am saved and sealed by the Holy Spirit

Eph. 2:4 I am loved

Eph. 2:5 I am alive in Christ

Eph. 2:10 I am God's masterpiece

Romans 5:1 I am justified through faith

Psalm 139:14 I am fearfully and wonderfully made

1 Corinthians 5:21 I am the righteousness of God in Christ Jesus

See what you are able to find. Have fun while doing it. It is so exciting to see how God feels about us and who He says we are verses what the world has said about us. I choose to believe God, after all, He is our manufacturer.

Take a few minutes and write some of the scriptures you find here:

____

____

____

____

____

____

While you're at it pause for a moment and ask God how He feels about you. Go ahead open your mouth and just ask Him. I did it a long time ago and He told me that He loves me. He told me that I belong to Him and He belongs to me. He told me that I am faithful, which I questioned because I knew that I had not been very faithful. He said that because I had been faithful over a few things He would make me ruler over much. When God speaks to you and tells you who you are believe Him. What He says to you should line up with His word. Now record what He says to you right here:

____

____

____

____

____

____

____

I hope you choose to make that Identity shift and crossover into kingdom. After all He has already seated you in heavenly places with Him. You might as well make the mindset shift and start living in the place where you are already seated.

You have to see the importance of studying the word of God and believing it and allow it to transform you. We as believers in Christ must begin to look more like the kingdom of God and less like the world. Jesus said He is the way, the truth and the life. It's time that we start doing it His way, believing His truth so that we can live life more abundantly. Remember who you are and what you have is and was always good enough.

We have a covenant with the Almighty through Jesus Christ. He is the mediator of the new covenant. Because of His sacrifice, we get to not only experience eternal life in the here and now but for eternity. Jesus paid the full penalty for sin. It's time to stop being so sin conscious and start living in light of who God says we are. We are the righteousness of God in Christ

Jesus. When we begin to understand our covenant relationship with God, we stop allowing life to just happen and start walking in the power and authority that He has given us. He has given us dominion and authority in the earth realm (Gen. 1:26-28; Luke 10:19; Matt. 16:19, 18:18). When we decide to make that Identity shift and crossover to kingdom we begin to see life so differently and we begin to walk more and more in the power and authority which He has given us knowing that He is always present with us. God never leaves us nor forsakes us. He transforms us and transitions us into who He created us to be as we stay connected to the True Vine. Are you ready to make that Identity shift and crossover to kingdom? I hope so because it is beautiful over here. This is my prayer for you as you continue your journey in Christ...

> *"that the God of our Lord Jesus Christ, the Father of glory, may give to you the spirit of wisdom and revelation in the knowledge of Him, the eyes of your understanding being enlightened; that you may know what is the hope of His calling, what are the riches of the glory of His inheritance in the saints, and what is the exceeding greatness of His power toward us who believe, according to the working of His mighty power which He worked in Christ when He raised Him from the dead and seated Him at His right hand in the heavenly places, far above all principality and power and might and dominion, and every name that is named, not only in this age but also in that which is to come."* (NKJV, Ephesians 1:17-21)

Made in USA - North Chelmsford, MA
1304799_9780578371085
02.14.2022 1745